A CONNOISSEUR'S GUIDE TO ANTIQUE

SILVER

A CONNOISSEUR'S
GUIDE TO ANTIQUE
SILVER

RONALD PEARSALL

SMITHMARK

This edition published in 1997 by SMITHMARK Publishers,
a division of U.S. Media Holdings, Inc., 115 West 18th Street,
New York, NY 10011.

SMITHMARK books are available for bulk purchase for sales
promotion and premium use. For details write or call the manager
of special sales, SMITHMARK Publishers, 115 West 18th Street,
New York, NY 10011; (212) 532-6600.

This book was designed and produced by
Todtri Productions Limited P.O. Box 572, New York,
NY 10116-0572 FAX: (212) 279-1241

Printed and bound in Singapore

Library of Congress Catalog Card Number 97-066056
ISBN 0-7651-9236-5

Author: Ronald Pearsall

Publisher: Robert M. Tod
Designer: Vic Giolitto
Art Director: Ron Pickless
Editor: Nicolas Wright
Project Editor: Ann Kirby
Typeset and DTP: Blanc Verso/UK

CONTENTS

INTRODUCTION

There are few who can resist the appeal of silver and its unique soft luster. Silver antiques mirror perfectly the period during which they were crafted. Silver collectibles are easily dated and identified, thanks not only to a meticulous hallmarking system—a marking system without parallel in applied art—but also because, historically, silversmiths were supreme craftsmen. These artisans were well aware of distinct fashion trends, which they readily applied to their craft.

Until the nineteenth century, silver was the domain of the upper classes. The variety, quality, and quantity of the silver they owned became symbolic of their affluence and power. In their efforts to flaunt their money, the rich frequently chose silver because to their minds there was nothing superior to it for function and utility. Scarcity and high price also helped to increase the status of this versatile, functional, and beautiful metal.

In 1870, vast quantities of silver were discovered in the United States, and in 1890 the duty on silver in Britain was dropped. The subsequent increased supply and lower price of silver meant that everyone, even the most humble, could have their cherished piece of silver. Silver had become democratised.

For collectors, silver is ideal. The variety and quantity available is immeasurable, and there are items to suit every pocket. All that is needed is a book of hallmarks and a dash of enthusiasm.

Right: A swing-handle cake basket of the Federal period, made in Philadelphia in about 1805-20 by Harvey Lewis, who died in 1835. The base has a robust individuality, marking it out as American; had this charming cake basket been made in the United Kingdom at this period there would be a heavier Regency flavour. Philadelphia was one of the great centres of silver-making in the United States; it was the third-largest city in the Union, exceeded only by Baltimore and New York.

Opposite: A silver christening mug and a pair of napkin rings. The ceremony has always been associated with the use and giving of small silver amongst the well to do, and mugs of this type have often been assigned on the basis of guess-work, as they could also have been used for more mundane purposes. Even including cutlery, the napkin ring is probably the most common of silver antiques, often bearing armorials and initials.

CHAPTER ONE

ABOUT SILVER

Silver is divided into two historical periods—from ancient times to 1870, and from 1870 onward, when vast quantities of silver were discovered in Nevada and the world supply increased tenfold. Before 1870 silver was a precious metal; after that it was not. The increased supply of silver made it possible to mass-produce silver-cased "workmen's watches" at low cost, and to make silver brooches for a few shillings or a dollar or two. This sudden availability of a previously precious metal revolutionised the way silver was regarded—though many did and still do consider silver to be something special, as evidenced when they try to sell some small, commonplace object such as a thimble to an antique dealer or through an auction house.

Opposite: An unusual type of antique—a spoon warmer in rococo style. The spoon itself is in the triffid style, a motif echoed on the thumb holder of the warmer. It might be asked why anyone should want to warm spoons, but when a dinner table was loaded with silver, the upwardly mobile members of the newly rich were at pains to display as much as possible, even if the objects had little practical use. The engraving is coarse and without a coherent purpose.

The Sterling Standard

In its pure state silver is harder than gold, but softer than copper. It is superior to gold as a conductor of heat and electricity, but is too soft to be used in its natural state and is therefore almost always alloyed, usually by adding a small proportion of copper. Silver will keep its brilliance until the alloy exceeds about one-quarter of the total volume. British sterling silver is .925 percent pure; the copper content is therefore much less than one-tenth. The silver standard varies throughout the world; in Germany, it is only .800 pure silver. In America, where silver is not fully hallmarked, silver marked "sterling" is .925 percent pure silver; "dollar" silver is .900 percent pure.

Below: A display of flatware, the name given to cutlery comprising forks, spoons, and sugar tongs. The term flatware indicates that the spoons and forks were stamped out in one action (knives were made by a different process). Until the eighteenth century it was unusual to find flatware in sets, and even the fashionable diner could find him- or herself presented with knives, forks, and spoons of different styles and periods.

Above: A tiny English silver-plated mug less than four inches high and said to be plated on paktong, an alloy of copper, zinc, and nickel. Paktong is a Cantonese (Chinese) word. Silver plating was a cheap substitute for silver, but was never really convincing except when the articles were new and unused, and even then the makers were forbidden to use silver marks under threat of heavy penalties. The makers of silver plate therefore used marks that looked like silver marks until they were examined.

Opposite: A Federal period coffee set made by the firm of Chaudron and Rasch of Philadelphia, which flourished from 1809 to 1812. It was custom-made for the Dallas family of Philadelphia and bears a crest and the motto LUX VENIT AB ALTO ('Light comes from on high'). In style it is a medley; the slop bowl has a base ill at ease with the bowl itself, and the finials of the sugar bowl and coffee pot do not match. The handle of the coffee pot is ebony. The cream jug has a refinement lacking in the three other pieces.

Above: The Ardagh chalice, a masterpiece of Celtic art in gold and silver. Ardagh is an ancient bishopric in Ireland founded by St Patrick, who made his nephew the first bishop in A.D. 454. In terms of style, this chalice is far superior to the ecclesiastical silver of the Gothic period, and works of this type provided inspiration to the artists and craftsmen of the Art Nouveau style at the end of the nineteenth century, especially the practise of studding the piece with roundels of precious and semi-precious stones.

Sources of Silver

It is likely that silver was not mined until about 4000 B.C., when the principal silver mines were in Asia Minor and the Aegean Islands. Gold was more common than silver in early civilisations, so silver was used very sparingly for jewellery and other precious objects. Silver was also believed to have magical qualities, and as such was frequently used to make objects that bore some mystic or religious significance. As the sun was associated with gold, the moon was associated with silver, and in later years alchemists gave silver the name Luna.

Silver comes from three main sources, in gold-bearing ores, in deposits of lead sulphide or galena, and native silver, rare and occuring in Mnorway, Canada, the United States, and Australia. The very rare "native silver" is silver in its purest form, occurring in Norway, Canada, the United States, and Australia. More often silver is found in ores that also contain gold, and in the more plentiful deposits of galena or lead sulfide. Electrum, a naturally occurring alloy of gold and silver, was often used by the ancient Greeks. Electrum jewellery was discovered when Troy was excavated in 1872–73, but the alloy has played no part in subsequent history. The precious metals of today are primarily gold, silver, palladium, and platinum, and are likely to remain so unless the supply of iron runs out.

The ancient Romans obtained most of their silver from Spain, while Austria and Germany served medieval silversmiths. Growing scarcity was relieved by finds in North and South America, now providing 65 percent of the world's output. When silver was scarce, large objects enjoyed enormous status; not surprisingly, most of these were connected with the church and not in private hands.

Above: A Regency wine cooler with characteristic swag decoration. Such formal decoration could be provided by embossing (hammering the design from inside) or by applying the swags in the solid and soldering on. Application in the solid allowed for far more detail and precision.

Opposite: The chatelaine was a clasp or brooch, usually of silver, from which various small objects were suspended by means of a chain. It was fastened at the waist, and was originally worn by the mistress of the house. Keys, seals, quizzing-glasses and nutmeg graters were among the items worn. This chatelaine is German and includes a penknife and a silver pencil. It is more elaborate than most.

The Price of Silver

The price of silver is often affected by its availability at a given time, but not always. With the discovery of vast new deposits in the 1870s, the price was five shillings an ounce (25p/40 cents), falling to under two shillings (10p/16 cents) during World War I (1914–18). Economic conditions played havoc with the price of gold and silver in 1920; there was an abundance of gold, and silver rose to 4s 11d (25p/40 cents), resulting in the debasement of the silver coinage (which until then had been real silver rather than the nickel and copper used today) from .925 to .500 percent pure silver. In the 1920s the output of silver increased, but the Great Depression in America and difficult conditions in Britain and Europe drastically reduced demand, and the price fell to its lowest in modern times—1s 2d (5p/8 cents) an ounce. The low price and abundant supply of silver generated a deluge of silver objects crafted in the new Art Deco style, which were available, for modest prices, to those not affected by the Depression. During this time, silver was regularly incorporated into such mundane objects such as cigarette cases and powder compacts. The low price of silver also pleased photographers, for whom silver nitrate was a necessity—there was once a fear that the demands of photography would deplete the world's supply of silver before the end of the century.

Opposite: A lattice workbasket with hinged handle and an escutcheon bearing initials. Perhaps it was used for cakes or sweetmeats.

Below: An elaborate Roman plate from the fourth century A.D., unearthed at Mildenhall in England, featuring a bacchanalian scene. The temptation with all show silver was to cram the object with every conceivable image, and this piece was greatly to the taste of silversmiths and the rich who commissioned such items.

By 1946 silver had gone up to 4s (20p/32 cents) an ounce, and silver coinage was replaced by silver-looking nickel and copper. Between 1951 and 1968, freak economic conditions—a world shortage compounded by devaluation in Britain—caused the price of silver to escalate from 6s 5d (32p/51 cents) to 18s 4d (91p/$1.45) an ounce. Price levels of antique silver became unstable, especially when the price dropped to 57p (91 cents) in 1972.

Testing Silver

There are several ways of testing silver. In the 1960s, when silver antiques were common and available to even those on a tight budget, "totters" and "runners" and

Left: A selection of fine small silver, including egg boiler, egg cups, casters, condiment containers, and sugar containers. It might be supposed that the egg boiler was a fashionable novelty, but when the distance from the dining room to the kitchen could be lengthy it made sound sense to cook in situ. *This accounts for many of the silver warming devices that found their way into the eighteenth-century household.*

Overleaf: Reliquary of St Andrew the Apostle in silver and silver gilt, set on a bronze base and containing over 200 gems, including six emeralds. It belongs to the Vatican and shows the skill, if not the taste, often characteristic of ecclesiastical art. Reliquaries were often architectural in design, with precious stones were added by worshippers—so many that the reliquary could be hidden by such stones. Reliquaries in the form of busts and limbs were made starting in the eleventh century and were very popular for four hundred years.

their children or urchin helpers (the lower orders of the antique trade) tested what they thought was silver by scraping it against a brick wall. If it was substitute silver (silver plate) it would show by exposing the base metal; if it was silver the scratches would buff out. In early times, there was no substitute for silver, or anything that looked like it.

Such unreliable methods have long been common. The only reliable, scientific method for testing silver is cupellation, which involves using high temperatures to separate the silver from any base metals present in the sample. The silver and base metals were then meticulously weighed separately and their proportions noted.

Above: Antique silver bowl, supposedly from Enkomi, Cyprus. Bearing in mind the legend of the Minotaur, its bull head makes it just as likely, perhaps, to have originated in Crete; however, the cultures of Greece and the Mediterranean islands were widely diffused, and extensive trading links often meant that this type of iconography was general rather than specific.

Hallmarking

Because of its great scarcity, silver was subject to vigilant hallmarking in Britain from as early as 1238. The leopard's head mark, applied by a punch, was introduced in 1300. The new standard mark, the lion passant gardant, was introduced in 1544. Both the leopard's head and the lion are derived from the Royal Arms of England.

The leopard's head, which was occasionally slightly altered, became the assay mark for London, while the lion became the national symbol of .925 percent pure silver. During fluctuations in price and quality, hallmarking was a sign of stability and certainty, and also of the prestige, even the magic, of silver. In eighteenth-century England, the devaluation of silver was a heinous crime. At a time when silver coinage was .925 percent pure and thus as good as bullion (silver in the raw), "coining"—counterfeiting using clippings from genuine coins melted down—was a hanging offence. In 1789 a woman named Christian Murphy was judicially strangled and burned for coining; hanging was considered too good for her. Coiners had their own ritual endings; the last coiner to be drawn on a sledge to the scaffold was hanged in 1827—ten years before the accession of Queen Victoria and thus almost in the modern industrial age.

As time went on, the hallmarking system became more detailed. Makers' initials were introduced, assay offices with their own marks were set up throughout the country, and date letters were introduced. Some of the assay offices lasted only a limited period: Chester assayed from the early fifteenth century, fully marked

Above: Silver-plate marks, which at first glance may be taken for genuine silver marks. They bemuse and mislead, especially when they have been encrusted with grime and dirt (often applied by unscrupulous dealers). They are not so close to silver marks as to get the maker prosecuted, though the head at the left of the series is not too far off the leopard's head of genuine silver. The initials with the head would be that of the maker. The other initials are either a private joke or applied with whatever punch was available at the time. Save for the drastic penalties for counterfeiting, there would be a great deal more silver plate masquerading as silver. Silver-plate marks that were intended to deceive were often applied in awkward places, such as across or near a join, to make identification even more difficult.

Opposite: A Greek silver and silver-gilt vase, or perhaps a form of amphora, dating from about the fourth century B.C. It is notable for the fine decoration and the lavish opulence of the curve of the handle.

Opposite: Embossed silver and silver-gilt table centrepiece with scallop-shaped dishes by D. T. Moye of Hamburg, dated 1633–44. This is a marvellous piece of incredible craftsmanship. The centrepiece superseded the standing salt as the prestige piece on the dining table and, in the form of a Victorian epergne, could be staggering in complexity. It is possible that the dishes were used, probably for sweetmeats.

Above left & right: Silver monograms were widely used, fixed with pins onto any suitable object, regardless of utility, and often found on dressing table sets. It may be that they served as identification, or that they were for sheer swank: a middle-class emulation of the armorial shields of the upper classes. Wood, as here, was the favourite surface. Over the years, they have often been prised off by the ignorant in the belief that, being silver, they have some value, which they have not.

1701–1961; Exeter, from 1701 to 1883; Glasgow issued some marks from 1681 and full marks from 1819 to 1864; Norwich from 1565 to 1702; York from 1559 to 1717 and about 1774 to 1856; and Newcastle, where goldsmiths reportedly worked from the mid-thirteenth century, had full marks only from 1702 to 1884. There are now five assay offices—London, Birmingham, Sheffield, Edinburgh, and Dublin. Everyday silver and novelties are most likely to be assayed in Birmingham, the mark of which is an anchor, a symbol decided upon by the toss of a coin.

Between 1697 and 1719, it was decided to adopt a higher standard of .958 percent pure silver, along with a new emblem, an image of Britannia. The Britannia image was sometimes confused with the Dublin figure of Hibernia introduced in 1730–31 as a duty mark. While the change was not welcomed, it was never formally repealed and silversmiths who wish to reinstate the Britannia standard are still welcome to do so. From 1784 to 1890, the sovereign's head in profile was applied to indicate that a duty (usually sixpence an ounce) had been paid to the government at the time of assay. At the Golden Jubilee of George V and Queen Mary in 1935 and the Coronation of Queen Elizabeth in 1953 the sovereigns' heads appeared again.

Above: A late Colonial period keyhole-handle porringer made by William Burt (1726–1751) of Boston shortly before his death. The porringer had been used in Britain from the early seventeenth century for porridge, possets, and other substances, and usually had two handles. The porringer was far more widely used in America, and the keyhole handle was essentially an American introduction.

Opposite: A standing cup with a nautilus shell mounted in silver gilt, made in Utrecht in 1613. The acquisition and display of rare objects in opulent surroundings became fashionable as the world was being opened up to the west, though these items were never intended as anything other than conversation pieces. Considering the early date of this piece, the quality of the silver is breathtaking.

Previous page: A collection of silver-gilt items of various periods. The ultimate purpose of gilding silver must forever remain a mystery, as the result is neither silver nor gold and, if anything, the silver is vulgarised by the process. The traditional technique was known as fire, water, mercury, or wash gilding. The mercury, dispersed in a vapour during the process, was responsible for the deaths of many silversmiths. The introduction of electrogilding in the nineteenth century solved this problem, as the process of electrolysis (the use of an electric current in a bath of gold solution) eliminated the danger.

In 1784, for reasons unknown, a standing Britannia was introduced for export silver. Lasting seven months, this export hallmark was a blip in a well-ordered system. The only parallel in the world of antiques is the system of registration on applied art such as pottery and porcelain, metalwork, and the like, in operation between 1842 and 1883 to denote the kind of article and the year, month, and day.

Standards in Europe varied considerably. France introduced a hallmarking system in 1275, but later used two standards, like the United States and Holland. The fact that there is no universal agreement leads to a great deal of confusion. German silver is not silver at all, nor is Nevada silver. The very simplicity of the English system left it open to such abuses as transposing marks from one piece to another to give an impression of greater age, or using easily made punches to apply false marks. The answer, of course, was to make such meddling a capital offence. The makers of pewter used imitation silver marks in the hope that the pewter, burnished and well polished, would be accepted as silver. This was a rather brave move, but since pewter was habitually recycled—resulting in its relative scarcity compared with the extent to which it was used—the risk was somewhat reduced.

A Versatile Metal

Silver is perhaps the most easily handled and versatile of all materials. It is extremely malleable, can be flattened into sheets finer than tissue paper (as in silver leaf), and can be built up into massive structures such as solid-silver furniture. It can be worked from the hammered sheet, moulded around a core, or "spun" in a fashion similar to pottery on a potter's wheel. Decoration can be embossed (punched from beneath), chiselled, chased, punched from above with patterns or designs, roughened, engraved, textured, and etched. This can be done manually or by machine as

Overleaf top: An example of modest embossed (repoussé) silver. Embossing, engraving and chasing (in which surface metal is gouged out with a sharp tool) are but three of the processes silver was subjected to. Silver could also be given a pattern by the use of different kinds of punches, and, being a soft metal, was most amenable for decorative treatment. Embossing was carried out from beneath by the use of various punches and other devices. A skilled silversmith could create delicate detail.

Overleaf bottom: Described as a Georgian sugar bowl, but because of the hinged handle, this piece could equally well be a basket. It shows silver at its best, the smooth lustre of the metal unbroken by extravagant ornamentation.

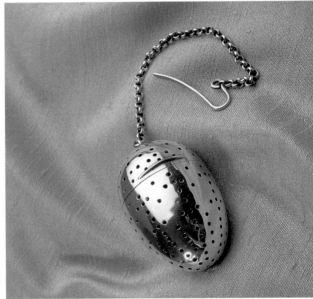

Above: A silver tea infuser, typical of a class of small antiques within the range of collectors on a modest budget. The tea infuser arrived late on the tea-drinking scene, when tea was so expensive that the ceremony became as important as the beverage itself. The use of an infuser would have been regarded as vulgar.

Left: Two French chocolate pots made in Paris by Joseph-Theodore Van Cauwenbergh in 1782 and 1784. The chocolate pot was similar to the coffee pot except that it had a rod topped by a finial in the lid so that the chocolate could be stirred. The handles at right angles were characteristic of European chocolate and coffee pots and were made of ivory, bone, or ebony to disperse the heat. These pots, with their wavelike bodies and sturdy, handsome feet, are typical of the best French silvermaking tradition.

in engine turning, giving an all-over pattern often used on small boxes or items such as watchcases and cigarette cases.

Where decoration is bold and lavish, casting can be used and the joints soldered. Die stamping of cutlery has been practised since the seventeenth century. Although silver can take an immense amount of handling, the prolonged use of the hammer can alter the molecular structure of silver, so the object being made has to be frequently annealed (brought to a cherry-red heat, then quenched in an acid solution). A planishing hammer is used to remove all hammer marks, then the surface is buffed and the final irresistible and incomparable sheen is attained by applying jeweller's rouge

There is nothing esoteric about the making and handling of silver. Even the most lavish objects are made using common sense. Silver is no longer a luxury limited only to the rich, and nineteenth-century silver is within the budget of almost anyone with an interest in collecting it.

Above: A Federal period silver ladle made by Chaudron and Rasch (1809–12) of Philadelphia, atypical of American silver work of the period. The ladle has a lip on each side, is crudely decorated with grapevine and ancanthus leaf motifs, and has an unusual twisting handle, possibly to give added strength. It is known that these silvermakers made unusual objects, and it is probable that this was made for a specific buyer to his or her own specifications.

CHAPTER TWO

EARLY SILVER

It has been estimated that fewer than four hundred silver articles, including small pieces such as spoons, survive in Britain from earlier than 1525, only a third of which is domestic silver. This is three hundred years after hallmarking was introduced, and though on the face of it the equation seems unbelievable, there are reasons why it is not. Until quite modern times silver was regarded simply as a commodity, and the concept of collecting antique silver would have been considered an absurd fad. In earlier times, silver that was not wanted or was out of date was melted down and used for something else, newly assayed and restored to circulation. Ecclesiastical silver was sometimes spared this indignity, but not often.

History's Toll on Silver Supplies

A very low proportion of this early silver is of Saxon or Norman lineage, not because silver was unavailable, but due to a variety of historic events. Silver was used to pay the ransom of Richard I (1157–1199) when he was held captive in Europe after the Crusades, and Edward III (1312–1377) was known to "borrow" silver from abbeys and monasteries. The Wars of the Roses (1455–85) brought further chaos. The biggest upheaval of all occurred when Protestantism replaced Roman Catholicism as the state religion; upon the dissolution of the monasteries,

Opposite: A pair of beautifully crafted Georgian candlesticks of the middle range. The most desirable candlesticks are those fluted in the form of columns, either in round or square sections, but this may be only a fashionable preference. Candlesticks are the most common items of large silver to be found (understandable when one realises that candlelight was one of the most common methods of illumination).

Below: A silver spoon of no great age or distinction, typical of the kind of small silver which can form the basis of a collection at very little cost. As there is a good deal of variation in flatware, it is difficult to make an interesting display of such items. Silver teaspoons may be bought for use, but they are less functional than modern-day specimens.

Above: An early two-handled lidded cup of the Colonial peri-od, with the armorials of the Philipse family of New York. Very rare and of a type only found in museums, this cup was made by Jurian Blanck, Jr. (1645–1714) in New York. The piece has strong European (especially English and Dutch) influences and it is evident that American silversmiths had not yet developed a fully distinctive style, though the curious scrolled finials have a decided individuality.

Opposite: The Lambard cup of 1578, held in the Draper's Hall, London. This is one of the most spectacular silver pieces of the period. Silver was used for prestige, and immense wealth was needed to acquire it. In design, English silver was far more tasteful than the furniture of the time, which com-pared ill with continental examples.

Henry VIII (1491–1547) seized the silver from the Church of England.

This was not all. Of all the silver in use, most was in the form of coins, and the dearth of coinage in the seventeenth century due to the English Civil War necessi-tated the melting down of most silver articles to prevent financial disaster and the utter collapse of the monetary system. After Charles II was restored to the throne, there was once more a demand for status silver. In 1697, the Wrought Plate Act led to a wholesale refashioning of worn or old plate. In retrospect it is remarkable that any pre-eighteenth century silver remains, but it does, and in considerable quanti-ties. However, major seventeenth-century silver commands hefty prices in the four-figure range. In 1984 a silver-gilt cup (plated with gold) of about 1680, seven inch-es tall, richly ornate, weighing thirty-one ounces, sold for £28,600 (approximately $50,000) at auction. At the same time a spoon from the same period would have been worth less than £300 (approximately $500).

Out of sentiment or through whim, ravaging monarchs did spare some pieces of silver. For historical reasons Charles I spared the Founder's Cup of Oriel College, Oxford, which bore a fifteenth-century French hallmark. Much existing silver was imported, and the silver styles of France, Germany, and Holland had an immense effect on the designs of English silver. This was not wholly beneficial, since English silversmiths were simply flowing with the tide of fashion rather than striking out on their own to produce something essentially national.

The character of early English silver is very difficult to judge simply because so much is now gone. Judgement must be partly based on church silver, which by no means always echoed domestic silver. Very little thirteenth- and fourteenth-century

Above: Early Colonial mustard pot made in New York by Peter Van Dyck (1684–1751), an example so rare that it is the only one known. Of ovate form with an S-shaped handle of a rather mean form, it is resolutely Dutch in influence, uncompromising and uncomplicated with a body almost devoid of ornamentation and a curious open finial. The only adornment is the gadrooned base. It was at one time altered by the attachment of a pouring spout, though this was later removed.

Right: It would be difficult to conceive of a more sumptuous display of silver-gilt than this table service provided for Grand Duke Michael Pavlovich of Russia. It was made in Paris some time between 1793 and 1820 and bears his monogram. Where price was no object, silversmiths could truly extend themselves, unfettered by the usual constraints of supply and demand. Russia looked to the west for cultural influence and spared no expense to obtain the very best, whether it was French furniture, silver, or architecture.

silver can be confidently identified as English, and these pieces are mainly in museums, especially the Victoria and Albert Museum in London. Ornament on such pieces is frequently derived from architectural motifs, often applied inappropriately though with the greatest expertise.

Not surprisingly, this early silver is often regarded as above criticism due to its very rarity, but there is no question that many of these museum pieces are cluttered, ill-proportioned, vulgar; if buried and later excavated by archaeologists they might well be declared relics of the Great Exhibition of 1851. If these pre-Reformation artefacts are compared with, for example, Roman silver or Dark Age Celtic and Anglo-Saxon silver, there is no doubt that they lack conviction, energy, and aesthetic appeal.

Symbols of Affluence

As with other types of antiques, each age has its prestige domestic piece. During Gothic times, in furniture it was the chair (lesser folk used stools); in silver it was the standing salt container. These containers established status, and grand establishments might boast as many as eight such items of various sizes. Fourteenth century examples came in the shape of animals, or sometimes hourglasses. In Europe, the

Above: The mazer was a medieval drinking bowl, usually gilt, formed from a turned section of burr maple and mounted with a silver rim and, occasionally, straps. There are large standing examples on high feet from Scotland and a few from England. Mazers were rare after the sixteenth century, and it must be asked why one of the most famous silversmiths of the twentieth century was called upon to make one. Omar Ramsden (1873–1939) specialised in individually designed pieces; he and his partner's first commission was a mace for Sheffield completed in 1899.

Opposite: Ancient Roman goblet, in silver with traces of gold in the rose-garland beneath the rim. Dating back to A.D. 79 (the erruption of Vesuvius) at the latest, this vessel bears skeletons playing musical instruments around its barrel; one holds a torch turned downwards towards Hades.

Above: An ivory and silver rattle, a fairly orthodox commission akin to a Christening cup and never intended as a plaything, but as a means of displaying conspicuous wealth. Utterly nonfunctional, it must be doubted that an infant would have found this object of any interest.

salt container was a "nef"—an ornamental object in the form of a detailed sailing ship. Rarities such as coconuts and later ostrich eggs mounted in silver also served as symbols of affluence and importance. These novelties escaped the pillage because of their small quantity of silver, as did mazers (maplewood drinking vessels on silver mounts) for the same reason. Consequently more mazers still exist than do other domestic items, with the exception of spoons, which also survived because of their low weight.

The spoon was one of the few domestic items with a genuinely English identity in the form of Apostle spoons. The trefid pattern with three points was popular in the late seventeenth century, though the longest lived was the fiddle pattern, still with us today. Silver spoons exist from about 1500 in quantity because they were the basic piece of cutlery, used long before forks became a matter of course. Until as recently as the 1600s guests brought their own cutlery to formal meals, so spoons were not made in sets until the end of the seventeenth century. About this time spoons were strengthened by a rib, called a "rat's tail," running from the end of the stem to halfway under the bowl.

Foreign pattern books were popular in the sixteenth century, including Geoffrey Whitney's *Emblems and Other Devices,* published in Leiden in 1586. Vredeman de Vries's *Architectura* of 1577 and similar books brought Moorish and other non-European motifs to the attention of British silversmiths, who were heavily influ-

Left: Early Colonial period beaker made in the Dutch style by Cornelius Van Der Burch (c. 1653–1699) and decorated conventionally with a shield and a blind trellis motif at the base. The engraving, 'Robbert (sic) Sandersen 1685', dates it nicely and indicates that it was a domestic piece, and not a church piece (church pieces in America were inclined to be similar in appearance to their secular counterparts, making them difficult to classify). Because of their simplicity and lack of sophistication, including ad hoc decoration, such beakers are frequently faked. It is to the good that early silver has an incomparable presence that is difficult for modern-day forgers to comprehend.

Below: A collection of silver spoons illustrating the variety available, including apostle spoons, ladles, scallop spoons, and one with a pierced stem. Of all the small antiques available, spoons are the most common, and even those of some antiquity, which are fully hallmarked, are reasonably cheap. Collectors should beware of forks, which are rarer, as unscrupulous people will convert a common spoon to the more collectible fork by taking out part of the bowl and flattening the rest, a simple process to one acquainted with silver technology.

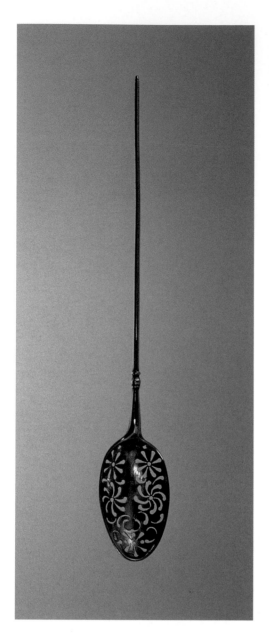

Above: An early Colonial mote, or strainer spoon, used to skim tea leaves from a cup of tea, made by Jesse Kip (1660–1722) of New York. The mote spoon had a long, unadorned straight handle, which served as a probe to remove leaves that had clogged up the spout of a teapot. The bowl was perforated, in this instance, with a flower petal motif.

Right: The Newdigate centrepiece made by Paul de Lamerie (1688–1751), one of the most famous silversmiths of all time. He was born in Holland of Huguenot parents, settled in London in 1691, and began independent work in 1712. He worked in the two fashionable styles: the stark, unadorned Queen Anne style and the heavier Huguenot style. This is a supreme example of the latter and impossible to fault; notice that the opulent ornamentation is an integral element and not grafted on as was often done in run-of-the-mill silver of the time.

Opposite: A James I wine cup of 1623, a handsome and elegant piece with somewhat eccentric decoration applied in an unsystematic way, especially below the rim. The stem of the cup is of great elegance. Silver is not ideally suited to the taking of wine, but the glass being produced at this time was cloudy, ugly, and of low quality.

Below: A plain tumbler and a discreetly ornamented bowl, typical of the mid-priced silver that can form the basis of a fine collection. Plain tumblers were made in large quantities, perhaps because they were portable and could stand rough usage. They were also easy to make by silversmiths not in the first league.

enced by the designs. Basins, tazzas (flat display dishes on stands or dishes on a base), plates with raised edges, standing salts, ewers, and other substantial domestic articles were covered with sometimes monstrous carbuncles in the form of sea monsters, masks, flowers, and almost anything that could be cast or embossed. Functional containers and drinking vessels such as tankards and beakers (the beaker, used since ancient times, was a development of the straight section of a drinking horn) partly escaped these excesses.

This florid era brought an increasing reaction in the seventeenth century, consolidated by the victory of Puritanism in the Civil War and the wholesale disappearance of huge quantities of old silver, melted for coinage or for recycling. The process resulted in a new form of ostentation, manifested in silver furniture, mirror frames, chimney furniture (such as low firedogs sporting flame shapes), chandeliers, candelabra, chunky angular candlesticks of considerable charm, and sets of large vases modelled on Chinese porcelain shapes, which at least promised a degree of decorum.

However, the overall ethos was that wealth should be flaunted with large silver

Above: An early Colonial period tazza made by Jacobus Vander Spiegel (1668–1708) with the top engraved 'Myndert Schuyler/b. 1672 d.1755'. The engraving was carried out long after the death of Schuyler, who was a prominent citizen of Albany, New York. It is a somewhat odd piece to act as a memorial. The tazza is regarded as a footed salver—erroneously, as it was originally a wine cup with a shallow circular bowl. 'Tazza' is its Italian name; it was known in France as a tasse and in Scotland as a tassie, a term now obsolete. This piece is Dutch in style. Its heavy gadrooned rims on both the bowl and the base, a favourite method of ornamentation, gave added strength to the bowl, which, being rounded and without rough edges, was easy to clean.

Right: A pair of Charles II lidded containers, perhaps from about 1670. The fact that they are unmarked is unusual for such large, imposing pieces, leading to the speculation that they were either Irish or were specially commissioned, which seems most likely because of the inscription around the rim. This may account for the heavy ornamentation comprising natural forms and shell motifs, as it was commonplace for the rich to be fond of extravagant decoration, irrespective of taste.

pieces. A typical example of dining table prestige items is the monteith, a lavish scallop-edged deep bowl used to suspend wine glasses in ice water to cool them. This also illustrates the increasing sophistication of eating habits—the correct temperature of wines is not a thoroughly modern obsession. A more restrained bowl, with a cover, was the porringer, popular in Britain and America from the seventeenth to the late nineteenth centuries.

Scottish and Irish silver was not very different from English silver, and a great deal of both were produced. In about 1690 there were twenty-five silversmiths in Edinburgh alone. Regional differences are evident; Irish silver, for example, was especially ebullient. Irish silver, as well as customised silver for grand families, was sometimes unmarked.

In 1685 Louis XIV of France revoked the Edict of Nantes, resulting in the inflow of thousands of Huguenots, French Protestants blessed with more than their fair share of skills. They established a thriving silk industry at Spitalfields in London, and brought with them silvermaking abilities of a sophistication unknown in Britain. Working in a heavier-gauge silver, they established new standards, introduced novel techniques (such as applying fretted silver layers called cut-card work), and instilled life in an industry stuck in the stylistic doldrums. Their work, and that of the British silversmiths influenced by them, coexisted with that of the traditional tradesmen who refused to alter their methods.

Above: A Colonial period monteith made by John Coney (1656–1722) of Boston. The monteith's scalloped rim provided a method for suspending wine glasses in cold water in order to chill them. It was also used as a punch bowl. There are two theories of how the name arose; the favourite is that it derives from a seventeenth-century Scotsman who wore a cape with a scalloped hem, though the Oxford English Dictionary speculates that it may derive from a certain Monsieur Monteigh. The name was coined in 1683. This monteith is one of the more spectacular, with lavish decoration on the upper part of the bowl, an elegant fluted belly, a gadrooned base, and sturdy handles projecting from lion masks. It bears the armorials of the Coleman family of Boston inside the bowl. Only three monteiths are known to survive in America.

Above: A George III inkstand comprising a gadroon-rimmed base with curious feet, a sprinkler (to sprinkle sand on the wet writing), a holder for quill pens, and a pot for the ink. The elegantly designed containers are funtional and easily cleaned.

The Effect of Social Habits on Silver Styles

A new, simpler style of silver was already appearing in response to the demands of a new culture. Less rigidly formal and more intimate than before, this new culture was one in which women played an increasing part, highlighted by the emancipated, sophisticated women represented in Restoration comedy. Society began to place increased emphasis on intimate eating and drinking and on an easy relationship between the sexes. Vying for status was commonplace at such gatherings, and the professional hostess was starting to make her appearance. Her success rested partly on presentation, and the silver she used played an important part in this.

The taking of coffee and tea was to provide a great source of income to the silversmiths. More than anything, the introduction of tea and coffee made entertaining

an art form with its own rigid rules. Coffee was a Middle Eastern beverage, reaching Constantinople in 1511, and the first coffeehouse in Turkey was established in 1551. England's first coffeehouse appeared in Oxford in 1650; the first in London was located in Lombard Street in 1652. A proclamation of 1675 attempted to suppress them as a public nuisance, but so outraged were traders and customers that the proclamation was annulled.

The Dutch brought tea to Europe in 1610, but until the 1650s it was used in England on only very rare occasions since it could cost up to £10 ($16) a pound (today £300/approx. $500). By 1726, however, seven hundred thousand pounds of tea were imported; in 1766 this figure had soared to seven million; the total doubled by 1792 and doubled again within ten years. Because tea was so expensive, teapots were very small. Tea was kept locked up in caddies, sometimes with twin compartments (one for green tea, one for black tea). Not only did this encourage a variety of porcelain wares and a wide range of silver containers and accessories, but also

Above: A pair of eighteenth-century coffee pots—one restrained in design with an elegant ogee-type handle, the other with fluting. Both are aristocratic pieces of great refinement. Some have argued, with good reason, that the teapot and the coffee pot show the craft of the silvermaking at its very best, unencumbered by the need to be flashy and extravagantly ornate. The women who so frequently used these items were unimpressed by the meretricious; they needed teapots and coffee pots that were easy to clean.

Above: The vinaigrette was a portable smell disperser, containing, beneath a grille, a sponge soaked with aromatic substances. Its first recorded use was in 1698. Ornament was restrained, and the box had no rough edges. The vinaigrette preceded the vesta box, which came into use in about 1839 (when the vesta match was introduced). During the 1960s and later, when vesta boxes were fashionable and commanded high prices, many vinaigrettes were converted. These conversions were acts of gross vandalism.

Above: Made by Jonathan Clarke (1706–66) of Newport or Providence, Rhode Island, this punch strainer bears the inscription, 'Jabaz Bowen Providence January 1765'. The punch strainer filtered out debris. This specimen is exceptionally attractive—American Colonial silver at its best. The handles were often ornate. This one has two handles; some have only one.

distinctive items such as the teapot.

In what might be termed the culinary revolution, changes in eating habits toward the end of the 1600s resulted in a new range of implements. In previous centuries it had been uncommon to eat outside the home in polite society, but by the seventeenth century eating establishments and a plethora of coffeehouses became extremely popular. Because of pilfering, owners of such places were reluctant to give their customers a chance to pocket eating accessories, so gentlemen (never ladies) dining out carried their own eating equipment, often in fitted cases. Many of these utensil innovations have remained, in or near the cutlery drawer, but many have been forgotten. Pocket nutmeg graters, dating from about 1680, are among these long-abandoned items. (Nutmeg was an important spice in earlier eras; in medieval times it was regarded as a medicine with magical powers, and in the seventeenth century it was issued as an additive to drink.) If the graters were silver, so much the better for impressing fellow diners.

The nutmeg grater is typical of a small class of useful antiques made in a multiplicity of forms, reflecting current styles and fads. Early nutmeg graters were contained in modest cylinders with scratch decoration. These were replaced by heart-shaped boxes, then acorn, egg, barrel, oval, and egg-timer shapes. Very elegant ornament was applied, especially as the eighteenth century got under way. Pull-off lids and hinged lids coexisted. Some graters were fairly large—up to two and a half inches long—so were more likely to be dining table pieces rather than pocket silver.

Another culinary antique contemporary with the early nutmeg graters was the silver apple corer, introduced about 1680. Like many other small articles of period silver they are sometimes not marked. Like a much later Victorian collecting area,

Left: This is a curious double-purpose sugar bowl of the Colonial period, made by Simeon Soumain (1685–1750) of New York, dating from the years 1736–45. The lid can be inverted to make a bowl or saucer. It was a marriage gift, and possibly a one-off. Stylistically there is a Chinese influence, both in the shape and in the inserted decorative cartouches. Chinese ware was at the time enjoying a vogue in Europe, thanks to the massive import of Chinese porcelain. It was often copied, first at Meissen and then throughout the world.

Below: Eighteenth-century sugar caster and pepper pot of traditional design with pointed globe finials, and contemporaneous. The caster was a step on from the sugar bowl. Sugar was supplied in lumps and was broken up by sugar nips. Sugar tongs, hinged or of the flexible type, were used to convey the piece of sugar to the cup, or wherever. A sugar sprinkler was necessary for sweetening dishes. Pepper was far more important in the eighteenth century than today, as it was needed to disguise the taste of food which, to say the least, was going off. There was no refrigeration except for ice, which was brought in at huge expense and usually kept in an icehouse built in the garden.

Above: A collection of fine candlesticks of various periods, including a chamber candleholder which—unusually—has been preserved with its snuffer and its snuffer attachment. Because of hard usage, snuffers are inclined to break off at the point where the handle is soldered to the base. Candlesticks have enjoyed a revival since World War II, as they are put to their original purpose rather than placed on show.

Previous pages: A delightful collection of everyday English silver objects of the type that can still be purchased at relatively modest prices. Toast racks are among the most common of household objects, some being very elegant. When buying, it is wise to check that all the divisions are in place and have not come apart from the base, where they would have been soldered (though it is a simple matter to solder back). Mustard pots may or may not have their blue glass liners present, but it is of small consequence as, if necessary, they can be replaced at small charge. Sugar bowls and containers should be examined to see if they once had a lid; a look at the rim will usually help.

silver buttonhooks, there is little variety in them.

Candlesnuffers in silver or silver and iron became popular in the late seventeenth century, though "snoffers" were used centuries earlier. Snuffers, which look like scissors with a box at the end, were either kept on a tray or held upright in a stand. Many were highly ornate, and the trays also lent themselves to extensive ornamentation. Snuffers were used well into the nineteenth century, when gas lighting and oil lamps made them obsolescent if not quite obsolete.

Snuffers are typical of small silver in that they are overequipped to do a simple job. It was considered too indecorous to put a candle out by the simple method of wetting the thumb and forefinger and pinching the flame out. They are also typical in that silver is not the best metal for the task—iron is much better.

Following the restoration of the monarchy in the seventeenth century, England was in a state of flux, and society reflected this. Religious problems still simmered; political maneuvering continued. Not surprisingly, the applied arts were not all of a piece, as exemplified in silver. Tasteless show silver coexisted with functional household articles exhibiting well-applied decoration, essentially the result of a struggle between English taste and European taste (often more heavily ornate) and between the old school of silversmiths and the French immigrants. But there are magnificent pieces from the time as well. From the middle of the century all over Europe and Britain, the fashionable gift to a bride from her groom was a silver toilet set consisting of up to thirty pieces, including a toilet mirror, often chased and engraved with mythological scenes. Most of these sets have been split up but a few complete sets remain as an example of the artistry that was possible.

European Influences
in America

In Europe, silver was international, with styles crossing borders. The demands of the rising merchant class were similar no matter in which countries they lived. Unlike ceramics, there were no arcane mysteries to solve; silver was silver, and new techniques —such as the Huguenot fretwork designs—were copied and emulated.

Fashions in European silver were closely shadowed by the growing army of American silversmiths. Since the eastern seaboard was occupied mainly by the British, Britain was the main influence. Efforts to find silver in Virginia had failed, so without any known silver deposits in the British colonies, silver had to be

Below: The armorial and decoration on this silver tea canister, One of Paul de Lamiere's more modest works, it is largely restricted to the upper and lower edges, with ample space between. This was characteristic of his typical Huguenot manner. The motifs are conventional, but the lay-out of the base, with its shell em-blem, is exceptionally tasteful. The handle, which acts as a kind of finial, is distinctive.

Right: A distinctive Federal period tureen and tray by Joseph Lownes (1758–1820) of Philadelphia, dating from the early part of the nineteenth century. It bears an unidentified crest of a mermaid with comb and mirror. An interesting feature is the pomegranate finial, not so much because of the choice of fruit (the pomegranate had been used as a decorative device since medieval times), but because of the way it is set at an angle. The lid of the tureen also fits the base, making this handsome piece a dual-purpose object.

Below: A highly individual American silver and tortoiseshell tobacco box bearing the arms of the Welstead family of Boston. The maker was Joseph Goldthwaite (1706–1780), and the box dates from 1730–40. Above the armorial is what appears to be a pair of squirrels, an unusual feature to find. The tortoiseshell serves as a backing to the pierced and engraved lid. Silver tobacco boxes are by no means rare, but the use of tortoiseshell with silver is an interesting variarion if one can accept the clash of colour. Brass and tortoiseshell (buhl or boulle) is a more attractive combination.

brought in. It was either then used as it was, or melted down and refashioned.

The Massachussetts Bay Colony was the centre of the silver trade. The first recorded silversmith was John Mansfield, operating from 1634. By 1680 there were at least twenty-four silversmiths in Boston alone. American silver was less decorated and more tasteful than the English models, and gradually native-born Americans evolved their own individual styles, with the accent on proportions, form, and craftsmanship rather than on decoration.

Unlike the British colonies, the Spanish colonies were rich in silver, which had long been used by the original inhabitants for everyday objects. Spanish colonial silver was very much influenced by Spanish silver, which in turn was often Moorish or Dutch in character. Dutch influences in the States lasted a surprisingly long time (as recently as the early 1900s, for example, a Dutch dialect was spoken in Rockland County, New York). New York silver combines English, French, and Dutch characteristics. French influences came largely through the Huguenots who had been forced from their native land, supplemented by the craftsmen who fled the French Revolution. The French created enclaves in Detroit, Mobile, and New Orleans, but they made the most impression on Canadian silver; with Quebec at the centre of the silver trade, they *were* Canadian silver. Being Roman Catholics, often staunch believers, they frequently created work that was ecclesiastical, and of the highest of standards. As in Europe, the course of eighteenth-century silver—the great age—was being charted.

Left: Nineteenth-century electroplated nut bowl made by the Wilcox Silver Plate Company (1867-98), with leaf and natural forms above a wave-form pattern and a realistic squirrel forming part of the handle and denoting its purpose. The inside is gilded, probably not for aesthetic reasons but for safety in case the silver wore through to the base metal, which might conceivably have been toxic. This bowl is replete with marks including Quadruple Plate Meriden Conn *and* Wilcox Silver Plate *as well as two crossed hammers in a circle. Electroplate was a fraction of the cost of silver, and the makers indulged in extravagant promotion to persuade buyers that they were getting value for money. The term 'Quadruple plate' is meaningless.*

CHAPTER THREE

CLASSIC SILVER

The eighteenth century was not an age of political stability. It saw the American War of Independence, the French Revolution, and the invasion of England by the Scots under Bonnie Prince Charlie. But if the only history of the era was supplied by applied art, this instability would be unknown. It was the classic age in furniture, pottery and porcelain, and silver. What now appear as momentous events of the time—comparable to the American Civil War, World War I, and World War II—often bypassed the vast majority of the people, who carried on just as before, with perhaps minor irritations.

The compulsory introduction of the new Britannia standard of .958 percent silver in 1697 made silver marginally softer, and therefore less strong. Articles assumed a slightly more robust appearance, and the additional cost was passed on to the customer. There does not appear to have been any stylistic change, though the necessity of using a different kind of silver with its own individual characteristics must have infuriated silversmiths, who could see no reason to change the long-established proportions. Nor could anyone else, except perhaps the bureaucrats who framed the new laws.

Opposite: A silver container with a swing hinged handle, a cut-out fretted design, and a gadroon-edged circular base with geometric decoration. Space has been left for an armorial or monogram. It has a blue glass liner. Usually the purpose of a silver item is evident, but where there is no documentary proof, common sense must prevail. Ridiculous attributions have been made, especially by auction houses who have to put something in their sale catalogues, and, as in law, these attributions tend to be enshrined throughout eternity.

Below: The Sons of Liberty bowl by Paul Revere (1734–1818), who was not only a national hero but an important silversmith. The son of a Huguenot silversmith, he served in the war against the French in Canada, though he is best remembered for his immortal ride to Lexington on April 19th, 1775, described by the poet Longfellow.

Eighteenth-Century Silversmiths

Many of the master silversmiths worked in all styles. Paul de Lamerie (1688–1751), born of French Huguenot parents and appointed goldsmith to the king, moved effortlessly between the plain Queen Anne style and the Rococo of the 1730s and later. He touched nothing he did not adorn, and his masterwork is said to be the wine cistern of 1719 (now in the Minneapolis Institute of Arts).

Few silversmiths are international figures, and even fewer have their portraits in national museums. But Paul Revere, best remembered for his famous 1775 ride that warned of the approach of British troops and heralded the War of Independence, also happened to be one of the best silversmiths in Boston, and his likeness now hangs in the city's Museum of Fine Arts. He was especially skilled in armorials, though these were dropped after the war as being too elitist and English. He specialised in applied masks on tankards and other objects, as well as pear-shaped coffee pots. One of his best-known creations was the Sons of Liberty bowl of 1768. Of Huguenot descent, Revere was a master of Rococo, which continued in America until about 1775 when neo-classical styles were all the rage in Britain. After the war Revere turned to the neo-classical in the English fashion. Supremely talented as he was in silversmithing, however, for years Revere had had to earn his living in publishing, dentistry, and picture engraving. He managed to die a rich man, not because of his silvermaking but because he founded a successful bell foundry.

Revere was typical of the skilled craftsmen of America. The newly formed United States had a small population, and silver buyers were relatively few. Revere was fortunate, like many recent immigrants of the period, in that he could turn his hand to anything and change course when the need arose.

Below: An octagonal teapot from the Colonial period, made between 1720 and 1735 by Peter Van Syck (1684–1751). It is of extreme elegance, almost completely unadorned, though the handle is a later replacement and is too thick. Teapots went through many stylistic changes; the octagonal teapot was quite short-lived, though it was revived in Victorian times. It possibly was reckoned too masculine by the women who dominated tea-party etiquette.

Silver Serving Pieces

Tea and coffee vessels, and those for chocolate (known today as cocoa), underwent many changes during the century, yet, unlike silver of previous ages, models that had become outmoded were not automatically melted down but remained in circulation. Teapots were small, and grew larger as the price of tea went down and the insatiable demand went up. The first teapots were pear-shaped; these gave way to octagonal teapots by about 1720, then bullet-shaped pots. Drum-shaped pots appeared about 1770, then ovals, often with fluted sides, which gave way to the square neo-classical form at the end of the century. Not only were these teapots functional; most were masterworks displaying taste and discretion in their decoration, and the changes in style reflected fashion rather than the need to improve utility. Many were based on Chinese porcelain objects, not necessarily those associated with tea. Chinese hexagonal wine pots were sometimes used as a model.

During the first part of the century tea sets were built up piecemeal; only later

Opposite: The wine fountain, consisting of a large silver urn with a tap, was made in the second half of the seventeenth century and the early eighteenth, usually in tandem with a wine cistern, a large oval vessel for keeping bottles in cold water or ice. Fountains were sometimes used for holding wine, but also for hot water to wash up silver vessels. Rare in Europe, they were not uncommon in Britain. The Queen Anne wine fountain pictured was made by Pierre Platel, an important silversmith of Huguenot descent who flourished from about 1699 to 1719, but the stand was made much later, in 1833, by William Elliott. He used a gadrooned pattern and managed to keep in period, a difficult task at the time; it would have been an impossible task twenty years later, when England was in thrall to the Great Exhibition of 1851 and all that it implied.

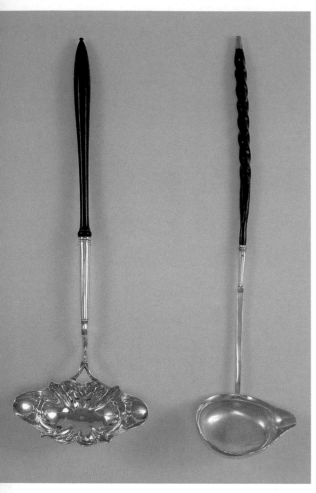

Above: Two American ladles separated in time by about forty years. The one on the left was made by Samuel Edwards (1705–1762), and the one on the right by Joseph Warner (1742–1800). The Edwards ladle has a wooden handle, the other of twisted horn. The Warner ladle features a bowl made from a European silver coin, a common practise before the Revolution. Both are elegant and functional, with their silver stems extending some distance to keep any liquid away from the wooden and horn handles. The twist in the horn gave the handle greater strength; it is a practise more often associated with wrought iron.

Right: Four magnificent George III candlesticks by Paul de Lamerie from about 1740, when the influences of the Rococo style, most often seen in France, were being felt in Britain. Sets of four of this quality are increasingly rare.

did silversmiths present the whole range of necessities as an ensemble. The tea table hostess would therefore have been providing "the cup that cheers but does not inebriate" from a variety of utensils of different dates. In any other medium such a presentation would have appeared anachronistic and out of place, but such is the nature of silver that everything matched. Kettles with stands, often with a spirit lamp to keep the water warm, were part of the ceremony, though the mahogany tripod table was later considered more chic for a kettle and its accompanying silver salver.

Coffee pots were taller than teapots, since the spout had to be well clear of the coffee grounds at the bottom of the pot. Whatever the basic shape, the pot sloped upward. Early coffee pots had the handle set at right angles to the spout, but this style was gradually dropped. Most British coffee pots and teapots had swan's-neck handles until the neo-classical period, when they assumed more geometric shapes, but European coffee pots often had a straight handle projecting at a right angle to the spout. The pots were broadly cylindrical or octagonal in shape, but the cylinder could be plain, fluted, spiralled, or somewhat bulbous, even pear-shaped, with embossed and cast decoration (very typical of mid-century Irish coffee pots). The lids were domed, plain or decorated, with a finial.

Chocolate (cocoa) was sold in coffee shops from the middle of the seventeenth century, and chocolate pots followed forms and fashions similar to coffee pots, except that the finial was removable or a hinged cover was provided for a rod known as a molinet, which could be inserted to stir the chocolate.

Accessories included trays and salvers, sugar containers, sugar nips in a scissors-like form (for sugar came in lumps), jugs, mote spoons (pierced spoons to scoop

Opposite: A classic teapot on a stand with its original spirit lamp. The stand itself complements the elegance of the teapot. One of the most appealing features is the position of the handle, though it was not especially functional as the steam from the teapot would have burned the hand of the person who was pouring the tea.

Below: It would be difficult to overestaminate the quality of this Paul de Lamerie wine cistern, with its marvellously executed grotesque masks both on the body of the cistern and on the terminals of the handles, and the successful combination of realism and abstract decoration. It is dated 1719-20, a time when the Queen Anne period was merging imperceptibly with the great Georgian age.

Above: A pair of eighteenth-century silver jugs, both of great charm, one with embossed fluting, the other with delicate engraving.

off floating tea leaves), and caddy spoons. Spring-back sugar tongs (such as those used today for cube sugar) date from about 1775. Milk and cream jugs followed the fashions. If food was served as well a beverage, the occasion might call for silver cake baskets, muffineers, toast racks, and, naturally, serving trays.

Formal dining encouraged the use of all kinds of silver, such as the argyle (or argyll), a gravy warmer in the form of a coffee pot, dating from about 1760. These and other warming devices were necessary because the kitchen was often a long way from the dining room. Dish rings (*not* table mats) were used to protect polished mahogany tables. Tureens of all kinds could be lavish and splendid, as could the ladles, scoops, and spoons associated with them.

Baskets and bowls intended for culinary purposes offered marvellous scope for adventure, particularly the baskets. Pierced latticework beautifully emulated wicker, with the motif repeated in the solid base. The handles—which either swung from central pivots or were rigid—often imitated twisted rope, and the rims were adorned with cast wheat ears, fruit, flowers, scrolls, and ribbons. Baskets and bowls were either round or oval; with the advent of neo-classicism they became either rectangular or octagonal. As the eighteenth century proceeded, bowls and baskets were set on raised bases. Bowls are one of silver's classic pieces, whether utilitarian or meant for display. In general, silver pieces with moving parts are less suitable to heavy ornamentation than are static items. Hence, where overdecoration might be inappropriate on certain silver items, bowls could support the added adornment because of their size and their basic simplicity of form.

Left: A Federal period coffee pot made by Joseph Anthony (1762–1814) of Philadelphia towards the end of the eighteenth century and clearly strongly influenced by English models, as is the case with Philadelphian silver. Although of traditional shape, it has one unusual feature: Whereas the body of the pot has little adornment, save for the modest repetitive design on the foot and the hinged lid, the spout displays extraordinarily bold—even fierce—decoration.

Below: Two novelty pieces—A George III cow creamer by John Schuppe, dated 1763; and a smoker's companion from 1877. Schuppe, a Dutchman resident in England, introduced this curious novelty once called a cow milk jug. The tail acted as a handle and the cream or milk came out through the mouth. The use of silver as the material for the cow fell out of fashion, but cow creamers were produced in quantity in pottery, the most rare being made by the potter Whieldon. Derby and Copeland made them in porcelain. Crude examples continued to be made by Staffordshire potters throughout the nineteenth century. The bear, by James Barclay Hennell, is alleged to have been a smoker's companion, though surely no smoker would want this creature as a companion.

Right: A set of two George II bombe (swollen) tea caddies and a sugar box by William Cripps from 1752 and a pair of inverted pear-shaped tea caddies with matching sugar bowl of the same period. The caddies—which would have held two compartments: one for green tea and one for black—are strikingly diverse; one is of mahogany with crossbanding and perforated silver applied designs, the other of leather, almost completely unadorned except for the escutcheon. Both caddies could be locked, as tea was expensive and servants were not unskilled in stealing tea and replacing the leaves with some concoction of their own.

Above: A complete eighteenth-century tea service of fine classical design. It is quite unusual to find a complete service in private hands and in such remarkable condition. This is English silverware at its very best, restrained and sophisticated.

Opposite: Silver wine labels are among the most sought after of small antiques and often command high prices. Originally called bottle tickets, they came into use in the mid-eighteenth century, replacing parchment or card labels. They were not obliged to be hallmarked until the 1790s. The most valuable are those bearing the names of unusual or obsolete wines or those with the marks of well-known silversmiths. The earliest labels were in shield or escutcheon shapes, followed by rectangular labels and, later, crescent shapes. Fancy shapes (vine leaves, animals, etc.) came in about 1820. Labels were also made in enamel. The Victorians re-created earlier models, but these are generally crude. The silver label was eventually superseded by the stick-on paper type.

Drinking Vessels and Related Items

Wine was mentioned as a medicinal cordial about 1300, and throughout the ages it was regarded with suspicion. Adulterated wines were seized and poured down the channels of the streets. In 1661 an act was passed to regulate the sellers of wine in England. Wine was variously taxed, and was also used as a political counter; in 1704 the Methuen treaty gave special preference to imports from Portugal and taxed French wines heavily. It is probable that the upper-class predilection for port dates from this time.

Wine drinking had its own individual silver. Silver wine cups, goblets, and other drinking vessels were less in demand after 1674, when Ravenscroft evolved a new type of glass in place of the cloudy, often stained and flawed, and easily broken soda glass. Wine glasses were initially based on silver models.

The most interesting object relating to wine drinking is the silver wine label, which replaced those of wood, bone, or parchment. Also called a bottle ticket or decanter label, it was suspended around the neck of the bottle by a short chain to denote the bottle's contents (adhesive paper labels were not used on wine bottles until the nineteenth century). Dating from about 1730, they reflect the increasing luxury of the age and the wide choice of wines available. The labels display the utmost variety and elegance, often crafted by the greatest silversmiths of the day,

Above: A charming and unpretentious lidded bowl with a formal design surrounding a space for an armorial that was never engraved. Armorials can be taken out, or even substituted for others, but it is not advisable.

such as Hester Bateman (fl. 1761–93). Until the Marking of Silver Plate Act of 1790, wine labels were exempt from hallmarking, though many makers added their personal marks. Early labels were handmade, but toward the end of the century Matthew Linwood and Matthew Boulton—a pioneer in the use of steam power in manufacture—used die casting; moulding was sometimes used instead. The sheer variety of shapes and lettering (sometimes engraved, sometimes cut through the metal) is amazing. The Wine Label Society has recorded 1,800 or so different names, though these include spirits, cordials, medicines, sauces, and toilet waters in addition to wines.

Tankards had been used from the 1500s, more often in pewter and other cheap alloys rather than silver, and they were customarily lidded. In the seventeenth century they largely escaped the piled-high decoration then in vogue, simply because this would have interfered with the tankard's function. During the Commonwealth, distaste for all things extravagant and upper-class led to an emphasis on drinking ale rather than the aristocratic wine, and also resulted in the tankard assuming a form that was carried on through the succeeding years.

With the increasing elegance of mahogany furniture—which showed the signs of casual usage more plainly than the oak and walnut that had preceded the mahogany age—it became necessary to prevent the bases of rough bottles from grazing the

Above: Early Colonial period caudle cup with a flared rim and S-shaped handles, made by Robert Sanderson (1608–1693). Caudle was a porridge-like substance mixed with ale or wine and often spiced. It was intended for invalids and ritually shared with visitors who no doubt enjoyed visiting the sick. Its name come from a word meaning 'hot drink' and dates from medieval times. The decoration on the bowl is somewhat perfunctory, but the handles are nicely done.

Left: It is rare to find silver being used as a vehicle for religious or political propaganda. This is an amusing example, a Colonial period beaker of the mid-eighteenth century by Daniel Christian Fueter (died 1785) bearing the message:

> *'Three Mortal Enemies Remember*
> *The Devil, Pope and Pretender*
> *Most Wicked Damnable and Evil*
> *The Pope Pretender and the Devil*
> *I Wish They Were All Hang'd In a Rope*
> *The Pretender Devil and the Pope.'*

The pretender refers to Bonnie Prince Charlie ('The Young Pretender') who in 1745 invaded England at the head of a Scottish army and reached Derby. The English retaliated by butchering the Scots.

Above: An ornate silver punch bowl with a highly decorated rim and a space left for an armorial. The naturalistic flowers on the bowl are well executed, and it would have been better had the rim been less fussy.

Right: A bold Federal period presentation cup with alternating acanthus leaves and anthemia as the predominant decoration. The oval cartouche is inscribed with the message: 'Francis Fredk McFarland/ to /Dr Hamilton/ as a token of Gratitude', and a flowing banner in Irish: 'Erin go Bragh'. The silversmith is Anthony Rasch (c. 1778—1858) of Philadelphia. Considering that it was probably made 1810—20, it has an old-fashioned appearance with a robust stem too substantial for the base.

surfaces of sideboards and tables. Wine coasters took a circular form, made of mahogany with green baize on the bottom. A silver button in the centre often carried armorials, and the silver gallery around the edge was usually pierced and decorated in the style of the day. Sometimes the coasters were made in sets. Wine that was corked or otherwise infected called for the use of a wine strainer, not unlike the ear trumpet in appearance. A strainer might also have two handles, to enable it to be stretched across a bowl when making punch, in order to keep out orange and lemon pits. Punch was drunk as early as 1632, though the first use of the punch bowl is recorded as 1692.

Above: Four wine coasters, by Eley and Fearn, of a surprisingly traditional design considering the date of 1823. This was the Regency period, when the applied arts were going through a transition. The coaster, variously called a slider, decanter stand or beerwagon, came into use some time before 1750 to allow wine, beer, and sometimes food, to be moved smoothly across the mahogany dining table surface. They were usually fitted with baize or small wheels.

The Rococo Style

The sparsely decorated octagonal, rectilinear, and circular silver artefacts of the reigns of Queen Anne and King George I have no parallels until the functional ware of the twentieth century. Though influential, the style was short-lived. The Rococo movement in France fostered a taste for frivolity and lightness, with airy scrolls, asymmetry based not on formal designs but on natural and plant forms, a sinuous grace, and a somewhat feminine informality.

Display silver such as candlesticks, centrepieces, and candelabra was ideally suited to Rococo. Candlesticks were once the favourite silver pieces collected, such was their variety. Centrepieces were designed to catch the eye of the diner; to reinforce their visual impact they were sometimes set on mounted mirrors. Centrepieces

Above: An epergne of the 1780s, that, although English, bears the crest of the Thomas and Johnson families of Maryland, and because of its odd shape was clearly a commissioned piece. The bottles and slender jugs are of glass with silver tops and, where applicable, silver handles. Although unquestionably spectacular, this epergne, with its range of holders for sweetmeats and other edibles, lacks conviction, and the tray holding the bottles is ungainly and ill-proportioned.

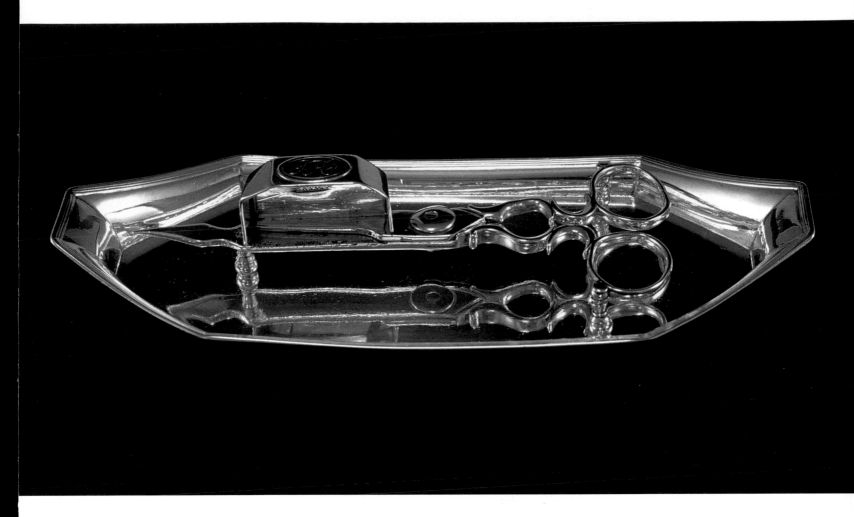

called epergnes were also functional, often fitted out with small baskets and containers and later with glass "trumpets" to hold flowers or other decorations. Candelabra had two arms until about 1770, at which point the number increased.

After 1740 most candlesticks had sockets to hold the candles; this helped to keep the hot wax from dribbling down the stem. Eighteenth-century candlesticks were usually moulded in three parts—sconce, stem, and base—using a lot of silver. Later in the century it was usual to employ rolled sheet silver, which was wrapped round a metal rod and was filled out with pitch or plaster of paris. This practise continued to be used, and could mislead buyers into thinking they were buying solid silver. This was also done with knives, where often the skin of silver was so thin that it fractured very easily.

Rococo appeared in all the applied arts. It formed the basis of what is known as "French furniture" but was never fully accepted in Britain or America (except in Philadelphia) because it was considered too pretty. Yet silversmiths realised that the sinuous and elegant motifs typical of Rococo were ideally suited to such basic silver objects as ewers, basins, tureens, trays, and salvers.

As had occurred in the late seventeenth century, the danger of overloading surfaces was ever present, particularly when fashionable styles such as chinoiserie (Chinese style filtered through European sensibilities), Gothic, and rustic were incorporated. Plain trays and salvers might have been redecorated in the style of the moment, causing confusion in cases where the date of the tray as indicated by the hallmark seems to clash with the type of decoration applied to the item.

An uneasy alliance developed between a watered-down Rococo and the increasingly important neo-classical movement, exemplified by the imposing work of

Above: Made by Daniel Carrel, a little-known silversmith, this candle snuffer and tray were made either in Philadelphia or Charleston between about 1785 and 1805. Snuffers were either of scissors shape, as here, or in the form of an elongated cone. They are relatively common and often very ornamental. Snuffers were initially placed in stands; the tray, either flat or with four small feet, was a later development.

England's greatest potter, Josiah Wedgwood (1730–1795), and in architecture by Robert Adam (1728–1792) and his contemporaries. In the 1780s and 1790s there was no contest: Purism had won, and even the most modest decoration was subject to stern scrutiny by the arbiters of fashion. Restraint was in fashion; it was not the time to be exuberant. Decorative sobriety had gradually returned to British design. Plain surfaces regained popularity, and heavy cast ornament was discarded in favour of the less obtrusive techniques of embossing, engraving, and chasing. These changes are quite evident in trays and salvers, bordered, as the new economy of decoration began to appear, with a gadroon edge, a little like piecrust.

Silver Boxes

Eighteenth-century changes in fashion can most readily be seen in the larger objects, and in small silver the readiness to adorn every surface with decoration was countered by the need to be functional. A box destined to be carried in the pocket,

Opposite: This rare Colonial period ewer, nearly twelve inches in height, was made in New York by Myer Myers (1723–1795), in about 1765. It bears the armorials of the Clarkson family of New York. Such pieces are not uncommon in the United Kingdom. Perhaps their relative disappearance in the United States was due to their being melted down for other purposes, especially in the years leading up to Independence. These ewers contained a substantial amount of silver.

Below: Of all small antiques, silver boxes offer the most variation, and although vinaigrettes can be very expensive card cases (introduced about 1780—before then, playing cards were used with the visitors' names written on them!), trinket boxes, patch boxes, match boxes and cigarette cases remain reasonably priced because so many of them were made.

for example, needed to be free of lumps and protuberances. Small silver was and is one of the most fascinating of collecting areas. Even collectors on a limited budget may find that their price range encompasses eighteenth-century examples of small silver pieces, many of which can still be used in the manner for which they were intended.

Whether meant for dressing-table use, desk use, or personal use, the dozens of different boxes for every imaginable purpose are among the most collectible of classic silver. Typical of these is the snuffbox, made in a variety of materials. The same types of decoration continued throughout the century, mainly engraving (sometimes engine-turned) and embossing, but not chasing because that process "lifts" the silver to form sharp (and therefore impractical) edges. The decorations display widely diverse content—sometimes initials, sometimes illustrations, sometimes armorials, and often intricate patterning. Silver boxes might have inset panels of agate, tortoiseshell, or mother-of-pearl and other materials. A technical feature that helps to date snuffboxes is the fact that prior to about 1740 the hinges were stand-away; after that point they were integral to the construction.

Vinaigrettes, which became fashionable in the 1780s, were small boxes with a grille, containing sponges soaked in acetic acid and aromatic spices to counteract the stench of city life and other people (rich and poor alike counted personal hygiene a low priority). The insides were heavily gilded to prevent corrosion from the vinegar. In later eras many vinaigrettes were converted into vesta boxes (match boxes), inherently less interesting.

Another small silver collectable is the etui, a small container with a hinged lid and separate compartments in which doctors carried lancets for use on their rounds. Similarly shaped and often of silver was the nécessaire, designed to contain scissors, needles, thread, and a thimble; or to hold cosmetic aids such as ear scoops, toothpicks, scalers (to remove tartar from the teeth), tweezers, and a perfume vial.

Opposite above: The Albert was a gold chain—with a bar at one end and a watch at the other—that was suspended across a waistcoat front, with the watch lodging in a pocket. This is a modern interpretation of what can be done with an Albert, invented in 1883 and named after Prince Albert, husband of Queen Victoria. Brass was often used for the mass market instead of gold. Amongst the diverse items on this chain is a vesta box for holding wax matches (far right). Vesta boxes came in all materials and shapes, some of them improbable and bizarre, and have remained a popular collecting field, perhaps because there is no question of what they were meant to be.

Opposite below: A toilet set usually comprises a brush, comb and mirror, and should carry a warning, as the silver is wafer thin and usually breaks, even if it bears a serious hallmark.

Below: A silver pin tray of no great consequence, but another example of small, agreeable dressing-table silver. Eighteenth-century dressing tables were without the range of small drawers that are a feature of more modern dressing tables, nor did they have fixed mirrors, but were topped by portable toilet mirrors that did have up to three small drawers in the base.

CHAPTER FOUR

THE STYLISTIC JUNGLE

The eighteenth century brought the Industrial Revolution, steam power, and a degree of mass production. The nineteenth-century silver industry benefited from reduced manufacturing costs, though the full value of the new techniques was not felt until the 1870s, when the price of silver dropped dramatically. Until then silver was still the province of the upper and middle classes; after that even the "improved" working class could buy a limited amount of silver, to the awe and bewilderment of their less affluent contemporaries.

Although certain processes simply cannot be done except by hand, most techniques were adaptable to machine methods. The first labor-saving device entailed the use of steam power to perform die stamping, turning out identical pieces such as forks at a speed that must have seemed phenomenal. Unfortunately, the encroachment of mass production led to an inevitable lack of individuality as machinery continued to churn out its identical items. Industrialization also brought with it a certain anonymity, and silversmiths, with their long-standing traditions and hard-earned skills, were in danger of eclipse by manufacturers who only wanted to make objects as cheaply and as quickly as possible.

Opposite: A superbly modelled knight on horseback accompanied by warriors on foot. The silvermaker was Robert Garrard (1793–1881), appointed royal goldsmith in 1830 and Crown jeweller in 1843. Best known for his solid but showy dining table, tea table and study ware, Garrard and the firm of Hunt and Roskell were the leading manufacturers of racing cups, trophies, and centrepieces. This truly magnificent piece, with a coat of arms on the base, was probably modelled by W.F. Spencer.

Below: Two knives, two forks, and two tablespoons of traditional design. The mixture of old and new flatware is considered acceptable. The silver on the handles of knives was often very thin, the core being of a pitch-like substance, and the weight is often deceiving. The shell motif is characteristic of what is known as the King's pattern.

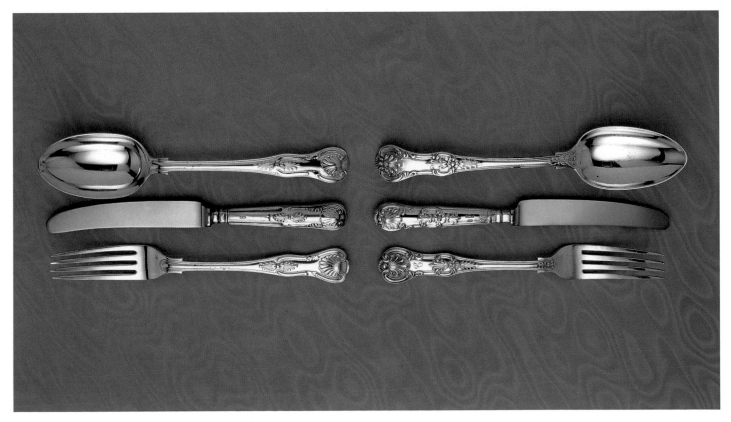

Above: A parcel-gilt (partly gilt) flask of the last quarter of the nineteenth century, with a radiating symmetrical design from a central circle, which seems to have been for a monogram that was not applied. The interior is gilded for safety reasons. Flasks were often kept in leather cases to avoid damage to the silver, and the decoration was always flat. The lid is both hinged and screw-on, with a leather washer to prevent leakage. The makers of this flask were Tiffany, more associated with their glass than with silver. Charles Louis Tiffany (1812 –1902), the founder of the firm, was a goldsmith and a jeweller, but a manufacturer and a vendor rather than a craftsman or designer. He began dealing in fancy goods in 1837, expanded in and assumed sole command in 1853, and in 1867, was awarded a prize at a Paris exhibition and opened a branch in London. In 1883, he was the biggest maker of silver in America. The glass which bears the Tiffany name was evolved by his son Louis Comfort Tiffany (1848–1933), a more considerable figure.

Left: A spectacular show of cruet sets, condiment containers et al. of various periods. Ornament, where applied, is formalistic and restrained, as these essential dining room accessories were not meant to impress. Some of the bottles are silver topped, others glass topped.

Warring Influences on Design

The century opened in some dishevelment. Conflict with France placed a heavy drain on the country's financial resources, and after the loss of the American colonies there was no ultimate guarantee, despite the apparent confidence, that Britain would triumph. But war in that era was never total war. Cultural links with France and the rest of Europe remained, and fashions and trends in the applied arts continued to be shared throughout Europe. New ideas brought forward by the Empire style of France were eagerly grasped, and sometimes improved upon in the English Regency style. Silver had gone through its period of exuberance in the late seventeenth century, and now, as the disciplines of neo-classicism began to fade (including the use of Greco-Roman motifs merely as added extras rather than as integral features of the overall design), a new portentous and heroic style appeared, offering echoes of that seventeenth-century exuberance.

Following Napoleon's systematic cataloguing of Egyptian antiquities, Egypt became the latest source of inspiration. His army had included talented artists, and their illustrations provided inspiration to furniture makers, architects, and potters throughout Europe. Silver was not so easy to Egyptianize, but master silversmiths such as Paul Storr (1771–1844) managed it with verve and assurance. The leading silversmith of his day, Storr provided silverware for the Prince Regent and other members of the royal family. After early work in the Greek style, he adapted his style to suit new conditions. He was especially successful in creating trophies and presentation plate given to generals and commanders in the Napoleonic Wars. When there was a demand for lightweight work he managed that too, and he died

Opposite: A Franco-American bowl with stand from between 1815 and 1825. Edward Lownes (1792–1834) provided the unadorned bowl, but the spectacular container and stand were imported from France and show Empire tendencies, most marked in the unusual terminals to the feet.

Below: An American salt dish of the mid-nineteenth century, made by the Gorham Company established in 1831 and still operative. The dish is small—hardly more than three and a half inches in diameter—but the work lavished on it is impressive, though retrogressive, as the sphinx motifs had long been discarded in Europe. Egyptian influences were never as important in the United States as they were in Britain and France, where they affected furniture, ceramics, and architecture (some of which survives, as in the catacombs at Highgate Cemetery, London).

before silver was caught up in a welter of conflicting and contradictory trends. He was not solely interested in "grand machines" but produced delightful miniatures, including enchanting beehive-shaped honey pots.

Regency silver was characterised by heaviness, emphasis on the horizontal, and a lack of lightheartedness, but silversmiths continued to hanker after the delicate and the frankly pretty where they could show off their ornamental skills. Though the return of the Rococo in the 1830s satisfied this yearning, it produced no real innovation, either in Britain or elsewhere. The style demanded traditional methods with less emphasis on the machine-made, but, talented as the silversmiths were, their creations have about them an air of the second-hand. All the stylistic tricks of the Rococo—the airy curvature, the emphasis on natural forms—were simply echoed without adding anything new. Consequently it is often difficult at first glance to distinguish between the originals and the reworkings.

The Revolutionary War in the United States had temporarily halted any innovative work, but at the beginning of the nineteenth century the work of the American silversmiths was as good as, if not better than, their European contemporaries. Although America too went through its periods of excess, the country continued to display an inventiveness with a distinctive American flavour. This was particularly marked in ecclesiastical silver, which followed domestic patterns and was often interchangeable. As the States spread west, new centres of industry were opened up

Below: A matching pair of sauce boats from the 1760–80 period, made in Philadelphia by John David (1736—1794) for Thomas and Sarah Cooch of Delaware. Commissioned pieces were often more adventurous than items for the shelf, and there is something extremely lively about the wide splayed feet and the formalised shell motif, which is soldered to the boat. Boats were regarded as multi-purpose utensils and were not always used for sauces.

by itinerant silversmiths who, often out of touch with European models, pursued their own individual styles. Some earlier silver manufacturers faded; Baltimore became one of the new silvermaking centres.

The reintroduction of Rococo in Britain was followed by an interest in Chinese and Gothic styles, though this time the pursuit of Gothic was genuine, even obsessive. The leading figure of the new Gothic was Augustus Welby Pugin (1812–1852). Though most famous for his designs for the furniture and fittings of the Houses of Parliament, Pugin was also a silversmith. Preoccupied with accuracy, Pugin took great pains to get the details right. He designed silver for the royal goldsmiths

Above: A pitcher of about 1804 by Paul Revere (1735–1818) of Boston, plain except for the inscription, which uses a variety of fonts very tastefully and effectively. It reads, 'Presented to the Revd. Joseph McKean, by a number of his Friends & late Parishioners of Milton as a testimonial of their affection, and to hold in remembrance how deeply they regret his separation from them. 1804.' It is a masterpiece of restrained silverware with a plain, perfectly proportioned, curved handle and a bold, uncompromising spout.

Rundell and Bridge, for whom Paul Storr and another important silversmith, Benjamin Smith, did work. Pugin also designed churches, and much of his silver plate was for High Church purposes. As a silversmith, Pugin was not important in his own right, but his influence was great and his books of designs and his emphasis on bold, solid, chunky forms was a startling change from the pick-and-mix efforts of his contemporaries who catered to the whims of the buyers.

Display Silver and Trophy Silver

The buyers of the nineteenth century increasingly included wealthy industrialists who wished to brag about their possessions, whether they were enormous houses, carriages bearing spurious armorials, or massive pieces of silver. It is often tempting to dismiss the nouveaux riches as tasteless, arrogant upstarts, but the truth is more complicated. Many encouraged innovation, many did have taste, and modern artists such as the painter Rossetti relied on businessmen as patrons. Display silver thus

Right: Mid-nineteenth-century candlestick made by Obadiah Rich (1809–1888) of Boston, heavy and lavishly decorated with what could perhaps be fox masks, a popular motif both within the hunting set and outside. The candleholder itself is supported by heavy foliate scrolls in a C shape. This has been described as an inkstand with the candle cup inserted at a later date, but as an inkstand it would have been absurd, as it is nearly seven inches tall.

could indeed be grand without being vulgar.

Closely associated with display silver, though more at home with the aristocratic set, were sporting trophies. Awarded in almost every sport (with the possible exception of sack racing), trophies found especial favour in the more upmarket sports such as cricket, golf, and particularly horse racing, which sometimes awarded trophies with horses and riders fashioned of solid silver. The trophies were often overwhelming; many of those that exist to this day have had additional names inscribed annually with the most recent winners. Sporting silver also included such small items as stirrup cups, which featured bases that were rounded or pointed so that they could not be set down but had to be downed at one gulp; these were sometimes shaped like horses' heads or fox's masks.

Large trophy silver was also made in quantity for officers' messes. Many of these objects date from before the nineteenth century, but the format remained much the same: made to be impressive and to celebrate the regiments' achievements. These pieces, usually containing vast amounts of silver, were often on permanent display. They were a source of considerable income to the makers and no effort was spared to give to those who commissioned them the very best. There was also a ready market for extraordinarily ostentatious display pieces that served a purpose, including silver wine cisterns, decanter holders, and claret jugs (sometimes in solid silver—there are some shaped like kangaroos, perhaps destined for the Australian market). It was common practise to recycle earlier display pieces by taking out previous ornamentation and coats of arms and replacing them with something more in keep-

Above: A gadroon-edged presentation tray with engraved radiating lines from the elliptical centre. It was presented to the Rev. R. B. Burkitt, M.A., by his parishioners on the occasion of his marriage , though, curiously, no date is mentioned. The lettering is early Victorian, though the refined, elegant, uncluttered style of the tray might seem to indicate that this was an earlier tray pressed into service for the happy occasion.

93

Left: A presentation set of silver napkin rings in a satin-lined box, a once popular wedding gift (greeted with muted cheers by the recipients). It may be chic to put two or three napkin rings on one napkin, as here, but it was a solecism. Nor did the napkins (never serviettes) billow out from the rings like a sailing ship at sea.

ing with the modern age and the current owner. In retrospect this practise is under-standable; silver was still considered no more than a commodity.

The Silver Industry and Public Taste

The desire to tap into the new middle-class prosperity—and the new overseas markets—came from the silver industry itself rather than from individual silversmiths. Few manufacturers had much interest in design; they probably kept only one designer on the payroll, and may have even shared that designer with another manufacturer. An object's basic structure was made by machine; the designer was required merely to add surface decoration—it did not matter what kind but the more eye-striking the better.

Numerous attempts were made to "improve" public taste. One of the earliest came from Sir Henry Cole, best known as the inventor of the Christmas card. Cole encouraged designers and manufacturers in the 1840s to raise their standards, with little result. Because Cole (along with Prince Albert) was involved in organising the Great Exhibition of 1851, he shares some of the blame for the plethora of rubbish that resulted.

For the Great Exhibition—the first of the international exhibitions—manufactur-

Opposite: A William IV presentation tankard by Rundell Bridge and Company, dated 1830, a magnificent piece associated with the Royal Yacht Club and bearing the name of the king and the royal coat of arms. It is replete with fascinating decoration, not the least of which are the cupids rowing shells on the frieze near the base. The lid is surmounted by a finely modelled lion. It is one of the rare pieces of show silver that successfully combines the formal and the informal.

Left: The Toby jug in silver is rare indeed. This one was made in 1886 by Andrew E. Warner, Jr. (1813–1896) of Baltimore. On the underside is engraved the legend: 'To Susan Dows Dec. 9. 1886 / from Enoch Pratt of Baltimore.' Pratt was a well-known merchant and philanthropist. The identity of Susan Dows is less clear. Toby Fillpot , a heavy drinker, was a fictitious character created by the Rev. Francis Hawkes. The character inspired a print, which in turn encouraged Ralph Wood I, the Staffordshire potter, to make a figure in about 1761. Other makers followed suit, and the industry has been carried on both in Britain and America until present times, the figures still being fairly popular. The modelling of the silver is good, though the face is more handsome than that of the quintessential Toby, who looks what he is—a bucolic drunk.

Opposite: An electroplated ice water pitcher of 1868 marked Rogers, Smith & Co. Conn, an unbelievable farrago of taste-less nonsense in the Egyptian style, engraved 'Sybil/ from/ Father' on the lid (we have no documentary records of what Sybil thought of this). The finial is a bust of Cleopatra, and the base displays four sphinxes. The sidepieces allow the pitch-er to swing from a central stud, which also acts as a pivot for the pathetic handle. But one cannot help but marvel at the cleverness of the manufacturers, especially as they were work-ing in electroplate, less tractable than silver.

Left: A condiment stand, called in America a 'bottle frame', made by William Gale and Joseph Moseley, who flourished from 1828 to 1833. It has a finial in the shape of an eagle above a cannon barrel and an American shield, which may indicate that this stand has military connections. The silver tops to the bottles were made by William Watson and Thomas Bradbury of Sheffield, England, and it is likely that the bot-tles themselves were English, on account of their supreme glass technolgy.

ers outdid themselves. Aiming primarily to upstage their competitors, they offered objects conceived on a vast scale and produced without regard to expense. Ornamental vases by such manufacturers as Elkington of Birmingham featured masses of human figures entwined with flowers, stage props, and wriggling decora-tion. If a vacant surface dared to show itself, it was topped by a finial.

A summary of contemporary feelings was detailed in the *Journal of Design* in 1849:

> There is no general agreement in the principle of taste. Every one elects his own style of art. . . . Some few take refuge in a liking for "pure Greek", and are rigidly "classical", others find safety in the "antique", others believe only in "Pugin", others lean upon imitations of modern Germans and some extol the *Renaissance*. We all agree only in being imitators.

John Ruskin, social reformer and writer, fulminated against the deplorable taste of

the age, but he was only read by the converted so his writings were therefore of little practical use. Slightly off the beaten track regarding silver is William Morris, who started his own design and manufacturing firm in 1861. Morris promoted handmade objects true to themselves and the medium and he scorned mass production, though he himself often cut corners in his considerable output of fabrics and wallpapers, the items by which he is best known today.

Of great significance was the Exhibition of 1862, which introduced the general public to the delights of Japan. Japanese designs were seized upon by craftsmen of all kinds as an alternative to the tired stand-ins for early styles. The long-term effect of the vogue for japonaiserie was to reduce the clutter of Victorian homes. Japanese styles had only a marginal effect on silver shapes, but were used in engraved decoration.

Opposite: An amusing attempt to conjure up a typical Victorian dining room table, which, as a glass of claret has been poured out, one presumably must take seriously. The centrepiece should be where it belongs—in the centre of the table. The tray is out of period, and, as claret is being served (the part-silver claret jug is evidence), it is probably a formal meal, for which the low-quality tablecloth is clearly superfluous.

Small Silver
Collectibles

The number of different pieces of small silver produced in the Victorian period runs into many thousands, and not surprisingly collectors find that they can build up formidable theme collections at little cost—items relating to drinking, eating, smoking, writing, needlework (not only the ubiquitous silver thimble), the dressing table, travel, clothing (buttons, buckles, and the like), and a dozen other categories. Since ordinary people now had more disposable income, they could afford little novelties that could be made as efficiently in a cheaper material. Writing accessories could include standishes with one or two inkwells, sealing wax ladles, wafer boxes, pounce or sand boxes (the sand brushed onto the paper to dry the ink), quill sharp-

Below: Victorian bone- or ivory-handled (or perhaps even composition) fish slice and fork in presentation velvet and satin-lined presentation case. The fish knife is the Cinderella of silver. No one wants them, few use them, and for a few pounds or dollars a collector could build up a comprensive, perhaps complete, display.

eners (before the advent of the metal pen holder and nib), silver pen holders (the earliest was the one-piece dip pen; the dip-and-holder was patented in 1808), fountain pens, and pocket pens and pencils. Propelling pencils date from about 1870, some in weird and dysfunctional forms, and among the less common items were wax taper holders (for use with sealing wax, before envelopes came with adhesive to seal the flap), and silver rulers.

The many varieties of spoons can form a diverse collection—tea spoons, dessert spoons, caddy spoons (the most ornamental), soup spoons, and others. Many of the earliest spoons have over the years been converted into the much rarer forks by taking out part of the bowl and making prongs. Other dining utensils are asparagus tongs, marrow scoops, and skewers, and all the various useful and useless articles connected with formal dining.

Because of their immense variety both in shape and decoration, silver card cases have always been collected. By the 1830s the process of leaving one's card was a rigidly controlled etiquette, and woe betide those who chose to ignore it or misunderstand it; they would not be asked back again. *Hints on Etiquette and the Usages of Society* of 1834 explained it all. The earliest recorded card case dates from about

Above: Escaping from the excesses of the Victorian age, this functional card case with an inner compartment for postage stamps is an example of multi-functional small silver. In many articles, subsidiary features were built in, often with scant regard for common sense. Such novelties are very collectable.

Opposite: A silver-plated egg boiler of classic design, complete with egg cups and spoons and completely free of decoration except for the spiralled roundels on the base. One can never cease to marvel at the high quality of even the most mundane and peripheral of household silver.

Above: An early Colonial period caster of 1690–1700, made by Bartholomew le Roux (c. 1663–1713) of New York, with a high domed cover, various shaped holes, an ornate finial, and gadrooning at the base and the lip of the lid. Unusually tall for a sifter (eight inches), it could be a descendant of the standing salts of early days, the possession of which carried great prestige.

Right: A tea-caddy spoon and a marrow scoop. The caddy spoon was made by Joseph Lownes of Philadelphia, and the marrow scoop is of Georgian vintage but unmarked, so it is likely to have been made in America, where there was no systematic hallmarking system. Caddy spoons were traditionally shell-shaped, as actual shells were used when tea was first introduced. Between 1770 and 1820 there was a vogue for novelty spoons in the form of jockeys' caps, Chinamen, animals, and hands, mostly used on the handle but sometimes on the bowls.

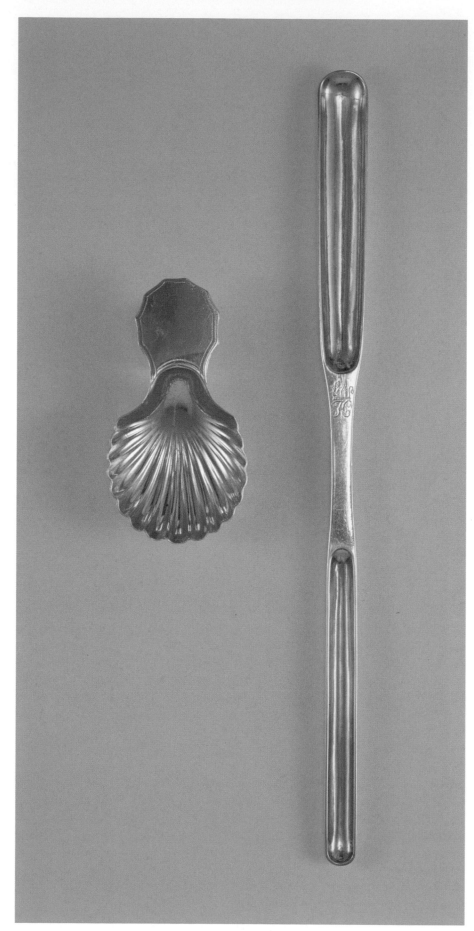

1820, though they were actually in use earlier. These types of articles were known as "toys" and their makers as "toymen." Birmingham became the chief centre for card case manufacture. Card cases often bear well-executed illustrations—houses, castles, cathedrals, and townscapes were especially popular, often with Rococo-style edging, like small picture frames for photographs and miniatures. The illustrations were usually in high relief, easy to stamp out in the thousands. Some bore Japanese motifs; with such a demand for card cases a certain degree of adventure was allowed.

The common factor of card cases is that they have no rough edges, and this is also true of vesta boxes, which are perhaps the most popular of small Victorian silver collectibles. ("Vesta" is an early term for "match"; the first friction matches were invented in 1827.) Vesta boxes, made in a variety of materials, featured a surface on which to strike the match, and a closely fitting hinged lid as a precaution against

Below: A wide collection of tea caddy spoons, both in silver and in the more rare mother-of-pearl with one novelty spoon featuring a camel. The caddy is of traditional design, though it has only one compartment instead of the usual two for green tea and black tea.

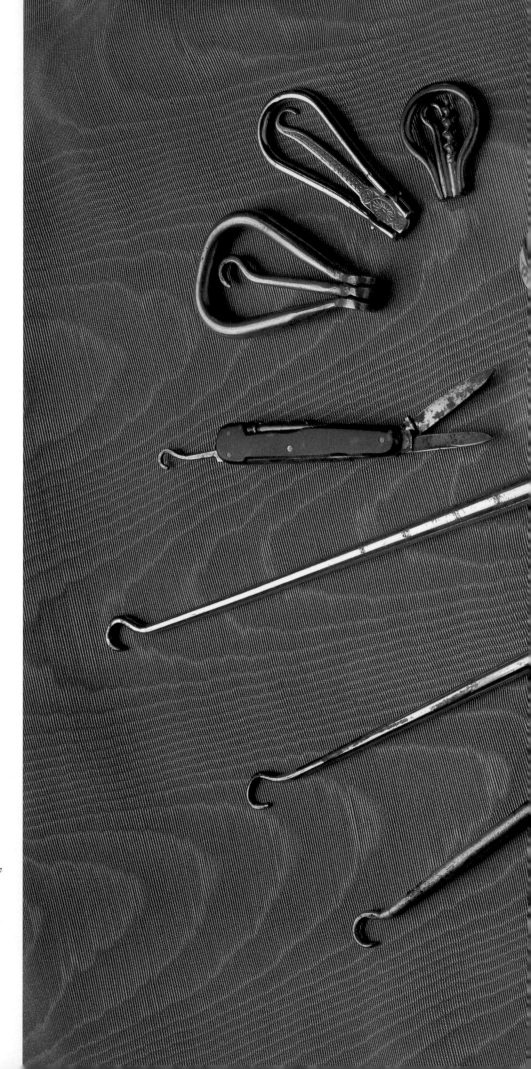

Right: A comprehensive display of buttonhooks, the purpose of which was to pull obdurate buttons through their holes, especially on women's boots, which is why the handles are usually long. Boots, it must be remembered, were standard footwear for the outdoors.

Following page: Visiting cards were introduced towards the end of the eighteenth ventury, and the ceremony of 'leaving one's card' became an elaborate ritual, to ignore the etiquette of which was tantamount to social exclusion. Salvers to receive the cards were also important—neither too extravagant nor so plain as to imply poverty. This example is perfect of its kind, with restrained embossed decoration at the base and scalloping on the edges.

combustibility. Though the classic silver vesta box is rectangular with rounded corners, silver vesta boxes came in all shapes. Some vesta boxes have double compartments and might be allied with other objects such as pocket knives, stamp receptacles, or cigar cutters. Intrinsically more valuable small silver boxes were adapted into vesta boxes, but these are easily spotted because the serrated striking surface is either absent or is unconvincing, an added extra rather than an intrinsic part of the design. Novelty boxes could include almost anything, even a compass on the side. The oddest box may well be the "Secret Photo Match-Box" of 1894, which opened to reveal a tiny picture frame.

As the nineteenth century drew to a close and the welter of styles proved intolerable, a new spirit was abroad. The efforts of the early anti-ornament pioneers were beginning to pay dividends.

Above: Silver boxes of all kinds existed in the thousands, both for indoor and outdoor use. Silver lent a certain status where other materials would have been as suitable, especially amongst the middle classes. Its cachet was lost on the upper classes, who always had silver around them.

William Morris were living in the past, that their abhorrence of mass production was out of tune with the times. Dresser, on the other hand, accepted the need for mechanised production.

Dresser's penchant for function and his austere preference for undecorated geometrical forms resulted in plain undecorated silver that was a generation ahead of its time. Much of it was unsigned, and is recognisable solely on stylistic grounds. One of the major silver firms he designed for, the Birmingham firm of Hukin and Heath formed in 1875, doctored and adapted Dresser designs to make them more commercial. Dresser was also art advisor to the firm of Liberty's, and some of their silver was supplied by the firm of William Hutton and Sons; since this often appears in the Dresser style there is some doubt as to whether it was actually designed by Dresser or was plagiarised by Hutton and Sons.

Fitness for function was the route ahead for Dresser and his apostles, and was to remain so for half a century, despite the efforts of mavericks such as the talented silversmith Omar Ramsden to muddy the waters by doing work of the utmost simplicity, as well as the effects of what can only be termed grotesques, as visually appalling as the worst exhibits of the Great Exhibition. Initially Dresser had few followers, but with the first flowering of Art Nouveau and a wholesale reevaluation of all aspects of applied art his work was seen as a wholesome rejection of the accustomed mess and muddle.

Opposite: An Art Nouveau vase of the highest quality, illustrating all that is best about the style, and why it is so sad that it was killed off, like so many things, by World War I. Amongst the qualities of the best Art Nouveau is a sense of intimacy, the use of a flowing line, and evidence of the pleasure of the silversmiths who carried out this work. The predominant feature of Art Nouveau was the use of plant and flower motifs, and the daring and bold embossing of these on the surfaces, with rhythms frequently echoed in the handles.

Below: Two visiting card cases of almost identical style, the one on the left being American (c. 1895), the one on the right hallmarked in Birmingham, Warwickshire, in 1894. The American case depicts the Philadelphia Waterworks in a raw, primitive style, the English case the Houses of Parliament. Both have excessive flowers, scrolls and leaves as extra ornament, and they belonged to a type of recklessly ornate small silver soon to be exiled.

Ashbee's Guild of Handicrafts

Opposite: An Art Nouveau silver hairbrush in inimitable style, with flowing plant forms, a pair of stylised birds, and the wavy, supple line that was displayed to such good effect in silver. The bulge in the handle is an interesting touch.

The late nineteenth century saw the creation of numerous small workshops, or guilds as they were often called. The most celebrated was probably C. R. Ashbee's Guild of Handicrafts, founded in 1888 at Toynbee Hall in London's unfashionable East End. Ashbee was a pioneer of Art Nouveau (though he did not like the description), and his work was exhibited widely, not only in Britain, but in Paris, Vienna, Munich, and Düsseldorf. His guild produced innovative Arts and Crafts silver, often incorporating inset semiprecious stones and occasionally mother-of-pearl. Unfortunately the guild was financially unviable and folded in 1908. In 1904 Ashbee founded the School of Arts and Crafts, which lasted ten years. In 1909 he published *Modern English Silverwork,* but he lost his faith and in 1910 he stated, "Modern civilisation rests on machinery, and no system for the encouragement of the arts can be sound that does not recognise this."

Ashbee's methods had failings that were to be the bugbear of adventurous movements. The workers were enthusiastic but largely untrained; this is apparent in some of the products, impressive at first glance but revealing serious technical flaws when examined closely. The early pieces were unmarked and unsigned, with a hammered finish and crude punched decoration. The better-finished work was probably designed by Ashbee and produced by more qualified silversmiths than those in his guild. Ashbee did not produce in great quantity, whereas Dresser did. And Dresser was always more innovative. Perhaps Ashbee's disillusionment with one-of-a-kind pieces and restricted editions was partly envy at Dresser's commercial success.

Below: A pair of ornate tongs carrying too much ornament. Allegedly for sugar, the presence of a variety of leaves suggests another more esoteric purpose.

Above: The ancient Romans enjoyed fine silver just as much as today's ardent collectors. Shown here are two beautiful silver double cups from the first century A.D.

Liberty Silver

In 1899 Liberty's launched its "Cymric" range of silver, the greatest achievement of turn-of-the-century silver. Though machine-made, Liberty silver was hammered at the end of the process to give a hand-finished look. Produced in commercial quantities by another Birmingham firm, W. H. Haseler, it was designed by the best people in the field, including Oliver Baker, Bernard Cuzner, Reginald Silver, Arthur Gaskin, Archibald Knox (the most important), and the surprise figure of the highly important Glasgow School, artist Jessie M. King. Liberty did not necessarily embrace fitness for function, but it provided the measure against which future silver was to be judged. (Seeing the success of "Cymric," many second-rate firms joined the queue, but luckily all Liberty silver is marked.) Cymric was a landmark, never to reappear, and the field declined thereafter. Although "Cymric" was made well into the 1920s, it began producing repeats rather than new creations.

To some collectors, Dresser, Ashbee, and Cymric represent the best of British silver since the vintage years of Queen Anne. Proof of this can be seen by comparing the cigarette case designed in 1903 by Archibald Knox for Cymric (now in the

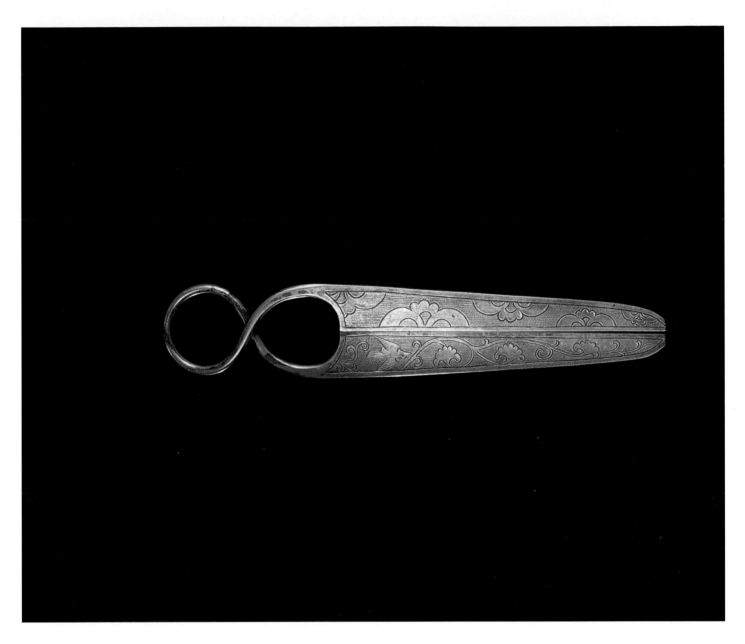

Victoria and Albert Museum) with the clutter and awfulness—all the worse for being immaculately executed—of Harold Stabler's 1909 loving cup in the same museum. Cymric was not the only producer of marvels; architect and artist Charles Rennie Mackintosh (1868–1928) created a silver presentation casket in 1909 (also in the Victoria and Albert Museum) that exhibits an elegance and originality on a parallel with his masterpiece of architecture, the School of Art in Glasgow.

Above: This pair of silver scissors illustrates some of the techniques introduced during the Tang dynasty from Persia. Made from beaten metal, rather than by casting, objects such as this were decorated with chasing, repoussé, and punching.

Silver in the Streamlined Age

World War I shattered all traditions. The immediate postwar products in any medium were vapid to the point of offensiveness, and only with the arrival of the pop, fizz, and vitality of Art Deco after the international exhibition held in Paris in 1925 were the applied arts worth looking at again. The whiz-bang streamlining of Art Deco lent itself well to plastics, ivory, ebony, and enamel but was not ideally suited to silver. In most items of the period (except modest jewellery) silver is coupled

with some other material. At times designers seem to have chosen silver only because of its prestige, not its suitability to the project at hand. Electroplate, silvered bronze (much used), and stainless steel—decidedly more jazz age materials—were generally more appropriate to the lines of Art Deco.

Certainly the Europeans and the Americans saw in silver something that could be adapted to this new style. Gérard Sandoz's silver tea service of about 1925 is a delight to behold, though its severe geometry casts some doubt on its utility. The tea service by Jean Puiforcat (1897–1945) of about 1930 is elegant, but decidedly impractical since the integrated spout has an aperture so small that it would block a tea leaf (there were no tea bags at that time). Erik Magnussen (1884–1961) produced an amazing coffee service in silver with oxidised panels called *The Lights and Shadows of Manhattan*. Peter Müller-Munk made use of Mayan and Aztec motifs. Georg Jensen (1866–1935), a Danish designer who hand-finished his creations, had a great influence on American Art Deco (though some of his work is a frightful combination of the old and the new and tends toward the distinctly creepy). American Art Deco is exceptionally attractive and adventurous in all fields, and the styling was used not only for art objects but for buildings, domestic appliances, and cars. Among adventurous American silver firms, International Silver, Reed and Barton, and Tiffany stand out, helped by energetic publicity.

Few British companies openly embraced modernism, and British Art Deco silver generally leaves much to be desired. One of the best-known designers, Scotsman J. Leslie Auld, sought his inspiration abroad, and was deemed good enough to con-

Opposite: British Colonial furniture pursued its own path, often combining British and local styles, as in this dramatic Indian chair in silver with traditional front legs and hoofed feet, unusual inward curving back legs, and reclining beasts as arms. The workmanship is superlative.

Below: The locket first made its appearance in 1679 to display a miniature or a lock of hair. It was usually elliptical in shape. With the arrival of photography and especially the carte de visite, a small photograph mounted on a card, in 1861, lockets were produced in huge quantities in all materials, with silver the favourite. These were affordable by almost everybody as the price of silver was low. The locket was fitted with a ring clasp for a chain and often worn by a woman around the neck.

tribute to the 1939–40 World's Fair in New York, a celebration of the future.

The concept of fitness for function coexisted with Art Deco, sometimes on a different plane and in a separate space–time continuum. The most important embodiment of this concept was the Bauhaus in Germany, founded in 1919 by Walter Gropius (1883–1969), who surrounded himself with gifted designers. Resolutely left-wing, Gropius was an undoubted genius, influenced by the English Arts and Crafts Movement, and a great propagandist. The movement's most controversial figure, the architect Le Corbusier, famously declared that "the house is a machine for living in." If that were so, then a cup was a machine for drinking out of, and a coffee pot was a machine for pouring coffee out of. Ornament was taboo. As a natural substance, silver was too idiosyncratic to be ideally suited to the Bauhaus style, but when it was used it was used superbly. Wagenfield's nickel silver tea and coffee set of about 1924 is a gem. After the Nazis closed down the Bauhaus in 1933, many of the designers went to America, where they continued their work for the benefit of the American public.

Fitness for function had a more modest effect in Britain. Herbert Read set forth its ideals in 1934 in his publication *Art and Industry,* which presented a civilised and persuasive history of functional design. His illustrations included everyday objects that were influenced by fitness for function, such as the white-enamelled, wooden-handled electric iron made for Marks and Spencer and the streamlined pull-along vacuum cleaner. Silver is mentioned only in passing. Hammering "is of course an absurd affectation, and contrary to all aesthetic principles." This is the reverse side of fitness for function—a rejection of everything that does not fit in with a rigid formula.

The Modern Age

Fitness for function was promoted in Britain throughout the war. The result was Utility furniture (after the war known as G-plan furniture) and the prefabricated house (the "prefab"). World War II dismissed Art Deco into oblivion; although it

Below: The handle of a buttonhook or something similar, with a tasteful inlay of silver on ebony.

Left: One of numerous dressing table containers, the hair tidy was introduced to keep the odds and ends used when hair styles were very elaborate. The hairpin was introduced in 1818. Some hair tidies, with apertures in the lids, were used as containers for the immense range of hairpins. This is a rewarding item for collectors, though the pincushion and pin holder are preferred.

survived in America after the war, in Britain and Europe it might almost never have existed, except as it remained in the form of debased chain-store examples in furniture, cherished odds and ends, and architecture. Fortunately many of the moviehouses of the 1930s survived as a potent reminder of what the style was all about.

The silver industry had witnessed a sea change: during the long years of postwar austerity silver was primarily used for jewellery (with gold for wedding rings). But the decline in the use of silver was partly sociological. As with all traditional crafts needing a stern apprenticeship, there was insufficient demand for master craftsmen to take on youngsters to learn the skills. Silver could be stamped out by machine, but the experts had to provide the input. It was much less troublesome to use old models rather than create new ones, if indeed silver was needed at all—there were so many more suitable alternatives. Status was provided by cars, clothes, or the neighbourhood in which one lived; with the decline of the aristocracy and gracious living there was no call for new prestige silver as long as there was enough traditional silverware to put out on holidays and special occasions.

As in all artistic mediums, one-of-a-kind pieces are still made by dedicated silversmiths for a select market. Hence there are still silversmiths. But in a rural classified telephone directory covering half a million people, there are three of them. In twenty years time, will they still be there?

CHAPTER SIX

SILVER SUBSTITUTES

The first substitute for silver was Sheffield Plate, sometimes called Old Sheffield Plate because it was the first of several forms of plating. In about 1743 it was discovered that a sheet of silver and a sheet of copper stretched at almost the same rates. If small amounts of lead and zinc were added, and the copper and the silver hammered together and placed on a surface, the two would fuse. There were snags: if the alloy was engraved the copper would show through. But the problem was solved with fly-punching, a process by which the silver was dragged so that it covered the exposed copper.

In 1765 came a silver-copper-silver combination, but it was too expensive. The aim of Sheffield plate was to make a cheap alternative, though manufacturers had no hesitation in adding imitation silver marks, a practise eradicated in 1773. Until 1784 there were no official silver-plate marks, but a law obliging makers to register a new mark in Sheffield was mostly ignored. Sheffield plate was never really suc-

Opposite: Except for Art Nouveau work, silver was losing its prestige, with silver tea and dinner services being replaced by more serviceable electroplate. At a time when silver is reserved for trophies and fripperies, it is salutary to be reminded of early silver work, when masterpieces were wrought with no regard for the laws of supply and demand. This parcel-gilt (part gilt) owl was made in Augsburg in 1630, and is perhaps a replica of a pet, judging by the collar at the neck.

Below: Sheffield plating, known in America as fused plating, was the mechanical application of a thin layer of silver onto copper, unlike electroplating, which used electrolysis, utilising an electric current to fuse silver to a base metal.

cessful because the copper always bled through. The edge of the article was vulnerable, though silver wire soldered on offered a partial solution. If a material other than copper is used the object is not true Sheffield plate. The proportion of silver to copper gradually dropped from one part in ten in 1760 to one part in fifty in 1840, and the result could be thoroughly unpleasant.

Mechanical silver plate was made obsolete almost overnight by the invention of electroplate, in which silver and nickel silver (copper, zinc, and nickel) were blended through electrolysis, using a bath of acid and an electric current. The prime mover for this method was George Elkington of Birmingham, who licensed out his patent all over Britain and Europe. With great skill he copied silver artefacts of all kinds, useful or frivolous; using electroplate he created new objects, often gargantuan, much cheaper than their silver counterparts.

Silver plate was within the reach of most. It could—and did—deceive, from a distance. Cheaper than electroplated nickel silver (EPNS) was electroplated Britannia metal (EPBM), an alloy of tin, antimony, and copper. EPBM has its supporters, but when the plate has worn the underlying metal is ugly, unlike Old Silver Plate, which wears gracefully as the copper merges mellowly with the residue of the silver coating. Britannia metal had been developed in the mid-eighteenth centu-

ry by pewterers, but it was never considered of great interest, although it was exported to America in bulk from 1816 (perhaps as revenge for the War of 1812!) until it was eventually electroplated.

Manufacturers welcomed electroplate, and it was used for mundane articles as well as artistic ventures. Electroplate was a favourite with Christopher Dresser and the advanced designers, and was much used in fitness for function designs and during the Art Deco period. The market for electroplate was limitless, and it has never been superseded except by stainless steel. Eventually the plate did tend to wear off, though manufacturers Mappin and Webb guaranteed their silver plate to wear like sterling silver for thirty years, and the best electroplate does seem to have a long shelf life. Electroplate has long passed from being a second-best substitute to a material in its own right. To purists it is still not the real thing, but collectors are warming to it. It is still possible to buy an electroplated display piece without mortgaging the house.

But there is no substitute for silver. It is the queen of metals, and those who have been bitten by the silver bug will never have a taste for imitations, however superficially convincing they may be.

Above: A pair of George III Sheffield-plated tea urns, traditional in conception except for individually styled feet. There are often handles at the side but these are replaced by hinged circular drops with a mask. The Greek key border would place it towards the end of the reign, perhaps around 1800. The term 'tea urn' may be confusing, as it was a hot-water container. It was an essential accessory, as bringing water from a kettle simmering on the fire would, as they say, have disturbed the ambience.

INDEX

Page numbers in **boldface** indicate photos.

PICTURE CREDITS

Ancient Art & Architecture Collection 14, 19, 20

Art Resource, New York 38

Blanc Verso 21

The Bridgeman Art Library, London 11, 18, 22, 24–25, 27, 35, 36–37,
42–43, 55, 62–63, 77, 111, 118, 122

Christie's Images 28–29, 39, 45, 46 (bottom), 48, 60, 67 (bottom), 68–69, 84, 96

Rosemarie Hausherr 6, 10 (top and bottom), 26, 31, 34, 36 (left), 41 (top),
42 (left), 46 (top), 47, 50 (bottom), 51 (top), 56 (top and bottom), 57, 61, 62 (left), 67 (top),
73 (top and bottom), 76 (bottom), 78, 79, 80, 87 (right), 88, 89, 90, 91, 92, 97, 98, 99,
104 (left and right), 110, 113, 123, 124, 125

MC Picture Library 7, 8, 12, 13, 15, 16–17, 23 (left and right), 29 (right), 30 (top),
30 (bottom), 32, 33, 40, 50 (top), 58, 66, 71, 74–75, 76 (top), 83, 85, 86–87, 94–95, 100, 101,
102, 103, 105, 106–107, 108, 109, 112, 114,115, 119, 120, 121

Minneapolis Institute of Arts 65

Museum of Fine Arts, Boston 59

Ronald Pearsall 9

The Pierpont Morgan Library, New York / Art Resource, New York 116

Werner Forman Archive, Eskanazi Ltd, London / Art Resource, New York 117

The Wright Family Collection 41, 44, 49, 51 (bottom), 52–53, 54,
64, 70, 72, 81, 82 (top and bottom), 93